RECORDS OF CIVILIZATION

SOURCES AND STUDIES

Edited under the auspices of the
Department of History, Columbia University

GENERAL EDITOR: W. T. H. Jackson, Professor of German and History

PAST EDITORS

1915-1926

James T. Shotwell, Bryce Professor Emeritus of the
History of International Relations

1926-1953

Austin P. Evans, Late Professor of History

1953-1962

Jacques Barzun, Seth Low Professor of History

Number XVIII
Tracts on Liberty, 1638-1647
In three volumes

THE WORLD IS RULED & GOVERNED BY OPINION

Engraved by Wenceslas Hollar, 1641

British Museum Catalogue of Satirical Prints, 272.

TRACTS ON LIBERTY

IN THE

PURITAN REVOLUTION

1638-1647

EDITED, WITH A COMMENTARY, BY
WILLIAM HALLER

VOLUME I
COMMENTARY

OCTAGON BOOKS

A DIVISION OF FARRAR, STRAUS AND GIROUX

New York   1979

Reprinted 1965
by special arrangement with Columbia University Press

Second Octagon printing 1979

OCTAGON BOOKS
A DIVISION OF FARRAR, STRAUS & GIROUX, INC.
19 Union Square West
New York, N.Y. 10003

LIBRARY OF CONGRESS CATALOG CARD NUMBER: 65-20968
ISBN 0-374-93401

Manufactured by Braun-Brumfield, Inc.
Ann Arbor, Michigan
Printed in the United States of America

Some years ago, while editing *Areopagitica* for the edition of Milton's works now being issued by the Columbia University Press, I undertook what I then thought would be a brief excursion into the pamphlet literature of 1643-1644. I was seeking a clearer appreciation of the contemporary significance of Milton's tracts. My conclusion was that what was really needed for that purpose was a critical survey of the literature of the Puritan Revolution in its entirety. The present work is offered as a step toward that end. I have endeavored to go systematically and with a fresh eye through the published writings of the period, using mainly the Thomason Collection in the British Museum and the McAlpin Collection in the Union Theological Seminary. I could not have done this without the help of others who have preceded me in the field (see the Bibliography for a list of the principal authorities used), but the selection of the tracts here reproduced, together with the accompanying discussion, rests throughout upon my own study of the original material. I have read much but not all, and no one could be more aware of the chances of error and omission.

The literature of the Puritan Revolution is important for its relation to Milton, but it is also of the greatest significance for much besides in our history and literature. Here, in a word, are revealed the beginnings of democracy, of economic individualism, and of modern English prose. Yet this literature, though it has been mined repeatedly in this direction and in that for one purpose and another, has never been studied as a whole for its own sake. Such study, at once critical and sympathetic, has been impeded by several causes. We have turned to the pamphlets of the Puritan age with a too-restricted interest in political history. We have been preoccu-

pied with single figures like Cromwell and Milton. We have
been the annalists and apologists of churches, sects and parties.
We have suffered from an attitude of condescension toward
Puritan enthusiasts and bigots as monsters of the mud from
which later generations have had the good sense to rise. But
the greatest difficulty has been the sheer bulk and complexity
of the literature itself. For coping with that bulk, we are now
equipped with the published catalogues of the Thomason and
McAlpin Collections, the latter excellent, the former usable
though far from perfect. The next desideratum, which we may
hope will before many years be supplied, is a catalogue of
English printed books for the period of the Civil Wars and the
Commonwealth, following the example of the existing short-
title catalogues for the periods prior to 1640.

The present work is intended to be of aid in another way.
The pamphlets here reproduced, printed as they are in facsimile, might have been issued severally. A number of important seventeenth-century works have lately been republished in
that manner by the Facsimile Text Society. But in view of what
has here been attempted, the present work has been included
in "The Records of Civilization," notwithstanding the fact
that that series has hitherto been devoted to the publication
of translations rather than to the reprinting of rare English
texts. Anyone who has attempted to follow the discussions
of the Puritan Revolution has learned that his practical difficulty, aside from that of gaining access to any considerable
body of the material itself, has been to select with confidence a
sufficient number of significant works and to interpret them
in their proper relation to one another and to the current of
the time. I have attempted to meet this need by bringing
together nineteen tracts upon the central theme of all revolutionary discussion from 1637 to 1647, the doctrine of liberty.
Each pamphlet presented was itself a significant part of that
discussion, and the entire number may be taken as a connected
series representative of the discussion as a whole. A running
sketch of that debate, with abundant references to other works

not included in these volumes, is supplied in the Commentary. Should the present volumes prove as useful as it is hoped they may, it will perhaps be possible, as it is desirable, to add others similar in plan, illustrating other aspects of the Puritan Revolution. One of these should probably be devoted to the agitation of the Levellers in the years 1647-1650 for a democratic constitution; another to the mystical agrarian communism of Winstanley and the Diggers; and a third to the autobiographical and confessional writings of Quakers, Ranters and the like, in which the work of such men as Bunyan and Defoe is so strikingly foreshadowed.

Some explanation of the arrangement of the present work may be useful at this point. The pamphlets reproduced will be found in Volumes II and III. Each section of the Commentary refers to one or more tracts in the later volumes, save for the omission of Roger Williams' *Bloudy Tenent* and of John Milton's *Areopagitica*, works which are already accessible to readers of the present day. The chief sources of information are the pamphlets referred to or reprinted in these pages, and all references are to original copies either in the British Museum or in the Union Theological Seminary. Dates of publication are generally appended to titles cited, old style dating being transposed to new without comment. The date of the month usually entered by Thomason on the title-page of each item in his collection is, as a rule, added in parenthesis. Included in the Notes in Volume I are brief explanations of historical and bibliographical allusions in the texts, but for full information the reader is expected to turn to the works cited in the Bibliography. The Bibliography is limited to the principal secondary sources.

The text of each tract in Volumes II and III has been reproduced by the photo-offset process without enlargement or reduction. A note accompanies each, identifying the original copy from which the facsimile has been made. No effort has been made to preserve the original size of page or width of margin, and defects, such as blots and discolorations of paper,

have been so far as possible removed. For all practical purposes, the reader is thus presented with a facsimile of the
original texts, literally faithful, but typographically cleaner
and easier to read than are the extant originals and, in some
cases, than the originals ever were. Certain difficulties nevertheless remain, difficulties which the reader can, however,
with some pains overcome. Several of the most important
pamphlets here reproduced were set up in the first instance in
a clandestine and hasty fashion. Paper was poor, type broken,
dirty and imperfectly inked. Authors frequently lacked access
to the printed sheets before publication, and proof reading was
either inadequate or entirely lacking. Lists of errata were
sometimes inserted, but the reader was also occasionally
warned of the advisability of making additional corrections
for himself, particularly in punctuation. The reader of the
present reproductions, in which the actual texts have been in
no way altered, has been left to follow this behest with the
aid of suggestions by the editor to be found in the Notes
in Volume I. He will find it useful to remember that the
seventeenth-century prose writer thought of the sentence often
less as a complete grammatical predication than as a full
logical and rhetorical statement of an idea which might require
a considerable number of clauses and more than one distinct
predicate. Roughly speaking, he seems to have regarded the
sentence more as we regard the paragraph. Of paragraph
indentation he made relatively sparing use. He was also sparing, according to modern habit, in the use of full stops. He
did, nevertheless, punctuate phrases, clauses, predicates and
other parts of the sentence according to his own conventions.
For this purpose, he felt free to employ almost any point of
punctuation, the comma, the semicolon, the colon, the mark
of parenthesis, even in some cases the full stop. He also felt
free to use any of these marks to register his notion of cadence
or emphasis, and to supplement them for this purpose by capi-
talization or italicization. Italics were regularly used for
proper names and book titles. In order to be at all effective,

any effort to emend such texts for the purpose of making them conform to modern practice must be carried to the point of complete modernization and so to the obscuring of historical aspects of the material which are of considerable interest and significance.

Barnard College, the Columbia University Press, and the Columbia University Council on Research in the Humanities have at various times assisted me to the leisure which has made my studies possible. The officials and attendants of the Library of Columbia University, of the Library of the Union Theological Seminary, and of the Reading Room of the British Museum have been unfailingly patient in serving my needs. My wife and Miss Sulamith Schwartz have been my most enduring assistants and my acutest critics. Miss Mary E. Knapp has supplied valuable help with proof and index. As the work has gone through the press, I have enjoyed the encouragement and sagacious counsel of Professor J. H. C. Grierson.

BARNARD COLLEGE   WILLIAM HALLER
COLUMBIA UNIVERSITY
    MARCH 15, 1934

CONTENTS

ILLUSTRATIONS

VOLUME I

COMMENTARY

The pamphlets of the Puritan Revolution have seemed to later generations like relics of a universe

> where eldest Night
> And Chaos, ancestors of Nature, hold
> Eternal anarchy, amidst the noise
> Of endless wars,

and yet those "embryon atoms" there engaged in elemental strife were the seeds of the modern world. Controversy in that great crisis revolved in ever-widening circles about religious questions which came to be not solved, so much as dismissed, or, it would be better to say, transformed beyond recognition. To attempt reform of the English Church in the seventeenth century was to attempt the reorganization of society. Dissenting religious minorities, one after another, seized the occasion to demand toleration for themselves, but the argument for toleration supplied ideas, terms and images with which men of any or of no religion might also contend for freedom of thought, of expression, of government and of trade. The religious doctrine of a supernatural law, and of a divine right vested in established institutions, evoked the rational or quasi-rational doctrine of natural law and of natural rights vested in the individual. Thus emerged the modern doctrine of liberty. But the religious and theological terms and images in which that doctrine took form did much to obscure the source from which it sprang. Religious freedom has set men free from religious or, at least, from theological modes of thought and expression, even when it has not led to the abandonment of religion itself. Religious dogma and religious passion, fostered by the high poetry of Scripture, undid themselves in serving to undo so much else. The eighteenth century, like many another true child, lived to disown its own begetters.

The scope of the present work does not permit more than brief definition of the sources from which the Puritan doctrine of liberty sprang. From the continent, perhaps from something deep-seated in the Anglo-Saxon folk, had come belief in the inspired character of individual desire and intuition. From Aristotle, from the church, from philosophers of the law, had come the distinction, so brilliantly brought to bear upon the English situation by Hooker, between supernatural law revealed in Scripture and natural law revealed to human reason in the material creation and in the heart of man. The age of discovery had opened to the individual mind vast vistas of exploitation and adventure. The Renaissance had glorified the human in art and literature. The English poets had rung unending changes on the Platonic conception of the One reflected in the Many and rousing the individual soul to action and expression. Under new conditions, these ideas recombined in new forms, found utterance with new accent and meaning. The narrow confines of London embraced an increasing multitude, whose needs and ambitions the old machinery of society no longer sufficed to satisfy. Uprooted from their ancient ways of life, men were plunged into the competitive intimacy of urban intercourse. There the church, as the exponent of beliefs and morals, found both a coadjutor and a rival in the press, grown cheap and prolific beyond the power of authority to control. Preached or printed under such conditions, old notions of natural law, of conscience and the inner light, of the One in the Many, took on a new function, supplying weapons to the many in their opposition to the intrenched power of the few. Hence it came that, upon the break-up of the old order, the many flew to utterance in the flood of publication which has left such heaps of now forgotten print, like burnt-out slag, upon the shelves of libraries.

The present work lays before the reader a series of revolutionary tracts drawn from the years 1637 to 1647. These were the critical years for the development of the doctrine of liberty. In 1637 the revolt of the pamphleteers against the Star Chamber called forth the dramatic defiance of Lilburne, recorded in *A Worke of the Beast*. The formulas laid hold upon by Lilburne, and then by Milton and Lord Brooke, for the attack on prelacy were carried forward by Parker in support of Parliament against the crown, by John Goodwin on behalf of the Independents, by Walwyn and Williams in defense of the sects, and were finally turned by Lilburne, Walwyn and Overton against Parliament itself. In 1647 they reached a kind of consummation in the Levellers "large petition," penned in all probability by Walwyn, and demanding an "Agreement of the People" which should serve as a basis for democratic government and an individualistic society. After 1647, the lines of the intellectual, as of the political, struggle were more sharply defined, and have perhaps been subsequently better understood. The democratic dogma announced in the "large petition," as Pease has shown in his admirable *Leveller Movement*, was fully elaborated by the Levellers in their unsuccessful attempt to win over the Army. The logical projection of that dogma into dreams and theories of a naturalistic communism was the work of that strange genius, Gerrard Winstanley. The defense of Cromwellian republicanism, idealized in the light of Greece and Rome, was undertaken by Milton. The sentiment of royalism was exploited by the *Eikon Basilike*, and absolutism was given a quasi-rational basis by Filmer, and a more philosophic statement by Hobbes. Popular discontent, finally, led by Ranters, Quakers and other prophets of the folk, ran out once more into the wilderness of religious enthusiasm and dissent. With these later aspects of revolutionary discussion, we are not here concerned. The great decision was taken when, in May, 1647, Parliament turned its back on democracy, which was the logic, if not the remedy of the revolution, and ordered the "large petition" burnt by the common hangman.

The reader of Puritan revolutionary literature must, of

course, be prepared to cope with modes of thought and discussion which in such connection are now obsolete, even when they are not repellent. Broadly speaking, the men of the seventeenth century thought of organized society as a religious body or church, with which the state was intimately and peculiarly related. The advancement of printing and the spread of literacy made the Bible above all the book, and theology the science, of the people. Consequently, discontent first expressed itself in religious terms. Liberty was conceived first as religious, and as appertaining especially to the church, and the doctrine of liberty was expressed in Biblical images and theological formulas. Thus Lilburne stands up as a soldier of Christ, converted to the true faith. Lord Brooke and Milton present the theory of liberty in terms of a theory of church government. Parker derives the social contract from the fall of Adam. John Goodwin lays hold of the Protestant doctrine of conscience as the justification for rebellion, Walwyn upon that of universal grace as the basis for democratic equality. But as the Revolution moved on, both the objects of revolutionary effort and the terms of revolutionary thought and expression, became less peculiarly religious and theological. This transition was no doubt furthered by influences that were not directly related to the Reformation. Brooke, Milton and Goodwin owed much to Renaissance Platonism and humanistic learning; Parker, Lilburne and Overton to legal writers such as Saint Germain and presently Coke; Walwyn to the English translations of Thucydides, Lucian, and Montaigne. Thus the argument that began as a plea for religious liberty and reform of church government rapidly extended itself to include civil liberty and political revolution, and the terms of the argument, so largely scriptural and theological to begin with, became increasingly rationalistic, naturalistic and secular. This transition in the modes of thought and expression, the present collection will be found clearly to illustrate. In order, however, to comprehend what happened, the reader must be prepared to endure patiently the intellectual habits of the age. His reward will be the recognition, attended by the peculiar interest that comes from meeting familiar faces in unexpected guises, of much that he may have regarded as of later origin. He will do well to observe a certain caution in the excitement of discovery. Our familiarity with theories concerning economic enterprise and political freedom can help us to find relevant meaning in the doctrines of election and of free justification without our having to conclude that Calvin invented capitalism, or the Antinomian sects democracy.

The pamphlets of the Puritan Revolution are also worth attention for what they reveal concerning the art of prose. To many modern readers, their style may seem difficult, obscure and forbidding, as indeed it not infrequently is; and yet in these pages modern English prose was rapidly taking form. At the beginning of the period, the stylistic methods of the pamphleteers were still largely derived from the schools. The learned and generally clerical writer, whether he preached from a pulpit or in a pamphlet, assumed a magisterial tone, expected to be heard with the respect due to his position, and confided in his command of an absolute science and an infallible technic. The result was that his discourse often degenerated into a jargon almost unintelligible at the present day, and also increasingly unintelligible, or at least unconvincing, to common men of his own time. These conditions naturally affected the style even of men of revolutionary temper like Brooke, John Goodwin and Milton, who also wrote not wholly forgetting the cadences of the Greek and Roman orators. But these men were affected, as Donne had been before them, by certain inherent possibilities in the very method itself when employed by vigorous imaginations. The syllogisms by which men trained in the schools derived working rules for revolution became poetic analogies. The text cited as an authority was used as an image, in which the revolutionary spirit could see itself mirrored in the life of the chosen and downtrodden, but ever uprising, children of Israel. Hence in the pages of Milton's tracts, and hardly less often in those of John Goodwin, not to

mention numerous other writers in this mode, are frequently
to be found passages of great beauty and power, obsolete
though they may be in style and structure.

Yet, though it is always possible, upon occasion, to overawe
common men by brandishing logic and erudition, it is also
possible to win them by the art of persuasion. The Revolution
called up a set of writers who had neither learning nor position in the traditional sense. All they could rely on for getting
a hearing was mother wit or, as they chose to call it, natural
reason, and they made a virtue of their limitation, if such it
was. They were plain men, speaking to plain men. They
assured plain men that plain reason was enough for the understanding and solution of all problems in church and state. They
preferred to cite no authorities, unless it were Scripture or
Magna Charta. What they said, they argued to be true because
it did not have to be derived from books, but was evident to
common observation and experience and could be stated
in common terms. They pretended to no language but the
vernacular, racy, concrete, apposite and emphatic. Lilburne
resorted to personal confession, autobiography and journalistic narrative and diatribe. Overton furnished, in addition,
robustious ridicule and dramatic allegory. Walwyn produced
a trenchant lucid English, detached in tone and often ironical,
which at its best would have been not unworthy of the eighteenth century itself. Thus the reader may note how, in the
very course of the Puritan Revolution, along with the hor-
rendous periods of the learned technicians, appeared that type
of popular prose which was presently to produce the master-
pieces of Bunyan and Defoe, and to exercise so determining
an influence upon English style. Even Milton abandoned, in his
latest tracts, much of the perfervid syntax of his earlier
pamphlets, and essayed as best he could a simpler mode of
writing.

One who reads the tracts of the Puritan period, attempting
to detach himself from traditional prepossessions, cannot fail,
finally, to see Milton in a new light. He will promptly discover

that the notion that Milton was in some fashion the initiator of liberal ideas cannot hold. What Milton did was to provide not the first but the finest literary expression to aspirations for liberty, expressed abundantly by other men whose writings were more congenial to contemporary minds. The men of the time read Bastwick's *Letany* and Lilburne's *Worke of the Beast*, not *Lycidas*; Brooke's *Discourse*, not *The Reason of Church Government; The Bloudy Tenent, The Compassionate Samaritane* or *Theomachia*, and not *Areopagitica*. Milton stood personally apart from the mêlée. He was known to few, and those few only such as he no doubt regarded fit, men like Vane, Lawrence and Hartlib. Before 1649, his pamphlets, in a time when pamphlet flew at pamphlet in almost unending rebuttal, went, it would seem, virtually unregarded. Even the divorce tract incurred chiefly opprobrium and little serious attention. Yet Milton is nevertheless, for us, the most significant voice of the age. He gave loftier, more learned, more ordered utterance to revolutionary ideas advanced by other men, utterance backed by erudition and intellectual power beyond the compass of most of his contemporaries, let alone contemporary revolutionaries. More than that, he fastened upon that one aspect of the doctrine of liberty which, however much it seemed to appeal in the circumstances of the moment to common men, appealed with peculiar force to the intellectual and the poet.

More than one influence from the past contributed to the faith of the Revolution in the power of words. The arts of ritual and drama, of architecture and graphic representation, were discredited by association with the oppressor. Scholasticism itself assumed that reason might be made to prevail, and truth be arrived at, by verbal discourse. The dispersion of the English Bible, however, gave to the hosts of discontent, uncritical as they were and literate only in the vernacular, an arsenal of infallible premises from which any common wit might expect to cudgel truth. Men believed that they could settle all questions under heaven by debate, if only they could be permitted to debate long enough. Few men active in the Revolution had any touch of Sir Thomas Browne's doubt in his own genius for disputation, or of his suspicion that a man might be in as just possession of truth as of a city, and yet be forced to surrender in an argument. The potentialities of such overweening confidence for the most gross absurdity and fanaticism, were, as Samuel Butler was to show, obvious and perhaps inescapable. On the other hand, the implications of such confidence in the advancement of spiritual and intellectual freedom were no less important. It was to the urging of these nobler implications of the zeal for discourse from pulpit, rostrum or pamphlet, that Milton devoted his genius. For him, moreover, the faith in the power of words was further transfigured by the Renaissance doctrine of poetry. His acknowledged master, Spenser, had written an epic poem, with the aim of fashioning men in noble and virtuous discipline. Sidney had defended poetry as the surest means to win the mind from wickedness. Milton was certain that the poet had office beside the pulpit to imbreed and cherish in a great nation the seeds of virtue and public civility. When he put off his singing robes, therefore, in order to write prose, he did so not for the cause of any sect or party. What he endeavored to achieve by his eloquence was an England so governed that poets might be free to exercise their office of freeing the people in mind and spirit, all other forms of freedom being without that vain. We need feel no surprise that his contemporaries paid little heed to this vision, or to the pamphlets in which it was conveyed. Milton, the pamphleteer, was still the poet. But the poet was for him but the apotheosis of the pamphleteer, and, for better or worse, something of the pamphlet was still to adhere even to his greatest poems.

M. Pryn Burton Bastwyck aen de pillorye
M. Prinne, Burton. Bastwicks in ye pillorye.

Meester Lilburn achter een kar gegeesselt.
M. Lilburne whipt after the Carts tayle.

PRYNNE, BURTON AND BASTWICK IN THE PILLORY
LILBURNE WHIPT AT THE CART'S TAIL

From England and Irelands sad Theater, January 10, 1645

British Museum Catalogue of Satirical Prints, 416.

I

THE REVOLT OF THE PAMPHLETEERS

JOHN LILBURNE

A Worke of the Beast [1]

The Court of Star Chamber,[2] in the spring of 1637, punished William Prynne, John Bastwick and Henry Burton for
publishing unlicensed pamphlets attacking episcopacy. Shortly
afterwards, John Lilburne suffered the same fate. These men
were by no means in agreement as to the limits to be assigned
to liberty. Nevertheless, by their dramatic defiance and suffering, they at once expressed and intensified that popular
demand for liberty which was soon to break forth in revolution. The circumstances were somewhat as follows.

Prynne [3] had long been a critic of prelacy and of the im-

---

[1] Vol. II, p. 1.

[2] The Stationers' Company had been incorporated in 1557 by an act of Philip
and Mary, conferring the exclusive privilege of printing and publishing books
in the English dominions on ninety-seven London stationers and their successors
by regular apprenticeship. No one could legally print books, unless by special
license, who was not a member of the Stationers' Company, and the Company
might lawfully search for and seize any books printed against their privilege.
Illegal printing was punishable by fine and imprisonment. In 1559, it was further decreed that no book should be printed without previous license from
the crown, the Archbishop of York or of Canterbury, the Bishop of London, or
the Privy Council. By a decree in Star Chamber, issued in 1586, the duty
of licensing books was vested in the Archbishop of Canterbury and the Bishop
of London, either or both, and it was the part of the chaplains of these digni-
taries to examine works intended for the press. Once a book was licensed, the
book-seller was required to register it with the Stationers' Company. Laud took
this part of his duties with great seriousness, and authors of offensive books
were tried and judged in the Court of Star Chamber, which was especially
concerned with whatever came under the head of sedition or contempt of
authority. A new decree of Star Chamber, issued in 1637, reduced to twenty
the number of printers authorized to carry on their trade in London. For the
arrangements made by Parliament for the regulation of the press after the abolition of Star Chamber, see below, p. 47 n. 39.

[3] For a list of Prynne's writings, see John Bruce's *Documents Relating to the
Proceedings against William Prynne in 1634 and 1637*, edited by S. R. Gardiner,
Camden Society Publications, 1872, and E. W. Kirby, *William Prynne*, 1931.

morality which he believed it fostered. He had assailed the wickedness of prevailing manners in *Healthes Sickness*, 1628. In *Lame Giles his Haultings*, 1631, he directly attacked the tenets and practices which Laud was attempting to introduce in the Church. In *Histrio-Mastix*, 1633, with an intemperance surpassed only by his pedantry, he assailed the immorality of stage plays, and of any who might be concerned in them as actors or spectators. This was at once construed as an accusation leveled at the king, queen, court and clergy. He was condemned in Star Chamber in the early months of 1634, degraded from his academic degrees, expelled from Lincoln's Inn, fined, pilloried, deprived of his ears, and sent to the Tower for life. To deprive the man of books and writing materials was, however, regarded by Bishop Laud as unchristian. Consequently, during the two ensuing years, Prynne continued, in defiance of the authority of the High Commission, to issue pamphlets attacking the bishops as violently as before. *News from Ipswich*, 1636, an assault upon Bishop Wren, supplied occasion for his second arraignment in Star Chamber (March 11, 1637), this time in company with Henry Burton and John Bastwick.

Burton, from his pulpit at St. Matthews in Friday Street, had also been a sharp critic of the bishops, and had finally taken the opportunity of a Fifth-of-November sermon to describe the arts by which, he claimed, the prelatical clergy were betraying king and people once more into the hands of Rome. With the pursuivants of the High Commission pounding at his door, he wrote out what he had said and dispatched it to the printer. It appeared as an unlicensed pamphlet, called *For God and the King*, 1636.

Bastwick, like Prynne, was already in prison. He had published two Latin treatises in Holland in 1633-1634, *Elenchus Papisticae Religionis* and *Flagellum Pontificis*. The Court of High Commission, taking offense especially at the latter of these works, fined him, excluded him from the practice of medicine, and remanded him to the Gatehouse until he should recant. But he, too, merely went on writing pamphlets against his persecutors. πραξεις των 'Επισκόπων *sive Apologeticus ad Praesules Anglicanos* appeared in 1636. Then abandoning Latin, he assailed Laud and the bishops directly in a series of short tracts, brought together as *The Letany of John Bastwick*, published in four successive parts in 1637.[4]

The three men were convicted June 14, 1637. They were fined, pilloried, shorn — Prynne for the second time — of their ears, and ordered for the rest of their lives to separate remote prisons. Their suffering occurred on June 30. Yet there appeared in London, almost immediately, *A Briefe Relation of certain speciall and most materiall passages, and speeches in the Starre Chamber occasioned and delivered . . . at the censure of those three worthy Gentlemen, Dr. Bastwicke, Mr. Burton and Mr. Prynne, as it hath been truly and faithfully gathered from their owne mouthes by one present at the said Censure.*[5] This pamphlet was an omen of the time to come. In its pages, the illicit press brought before the London populace the scenes, characters and very words of the drama which had just taken place in Star Chamber and Palace Yard. Almost the first act of the Long Parliament, when it assembled in 1640, was to release the heroes of that occasion. They were brought home from their prisons in triumph, and fell to again in the war of pamphlets against prelates. Prynne published an account of his martyrdom in *A New Discovery of the Prelates Tyranny*, 1641, Bastwick *The Confession of the faithfull Witnesse of Christ*, 1641, and Burton a *Narration Of The Life of Mr. Henry Burton*, 1643. Prynne further pursued the fallen primate in his *Breviate of the Life of William Laud*, 1644, *Hidden Workes of Darkenes Brought to Publike Light*, 1645, and *Canterburies Doome*, 1646.

Between Bastwick's *Letany* and the other tracts which so offended the authorities, there is a significant difference. The

---

[4] Reprinted in the *Somers Tracts*.

[5] Incorporated as part of Prynne's *New Discovery of the Prelates Tyranny*. It is also reprinted in the *Harleian Miscellany*, and forms the basis for the account of the proceedings given in *State Trials*.

others professed, at least, to persuade the reader by a display
of the type of logic and erudition which most men accepted as
the idiom of truth, even when they could not understand it.
Bastwick's *Letany* was written, not to impress but to rouse,
and not the educated but the unlearned. The friends who came
to see the author in the Gatehouse had urged him to write
something against bishops which would appeal to people who
could read nothing but English. Bastwick was thus led to com-
pose his *Letany*. Sacrificing dialectic and learning for language
that would directly evoke, in the minds of the discontented
populace, the image of what they hated, he sought to stir
laughter, contempt and anger. The book, he says

will be a great help to stirre up in thee a Christian hatred, not onely
of the great beast that came out of the sea, and all the abominations and
monstruous impietyes that come ratified *sub sigillo piscatoris*, but also a
pious zeale and fervent indignation against all the damnable inventions &
barterings of all those Fishmongers, that have bought and sold Christs
best fishes through town and country these many generations like red
herrings, sprats and poore Iohns, and made them the mundungus
and garbridge both of sea and land and the offscourings of all things,
which the Lord of life notwithstanding bought with no lesse price then
with his owne most blessed and precious bloud. And as it will breed in
thee a holy indignation, against all their wicked crueltyes and attempts,
so likewise I doubt not, it will move thee with a concatenated unanimity
to joyne with all those that wish the peace of Jerusalem and desolation of
Babilon in our dayly *letany*, praying from *plague, pestilence and famine,
from Bishops, Priests and Deacons, good Lord deliver us.*

Letany, Part I, 10.

The *Letany* pleased its author's friends. Passing in manu-
script from hand to hand, it attracted fresh visitors to his
room in prison. Among these was a young man hardly out of
his apprenticeship, whose imagination had been stirred by the
conspicuous self-devotion of Bastwick and Prynne. His name
was John Lilburne, and he was, it would seem, though the
accounts are somewhat confused, about to go to Holland
in the hope of setting up in trade. When he arrived in Holland
a little later, he probably had with him a copy of the *Letany*.

At any rate, he was presently accused of printing that and other seditious tracts in Rotterdam, and of shipping them back to England for sale. The English authorities arrested Lilburne's confederate, who gave up the secret to save his own skin. At least one shipment of the *Letany* was in consequence seized, and then Lilburne himself upon his return in December, 1637. Brought before Star Chamber on the charge of printing and circulating unlicensed books, he refused to take the "ex Officio" oath on the ground that it would bind him to answer incriminating questions. He was convicted and sentenced, February 13, 1638, and on the eighteenth of April he was punished in the manner he himself describes.

In the example of Prynne, Burton and Bastwick, in the racy vigor of Bastwick's *Letany*, and in the journalistic effectiveness of *A Briefe Relation*, Lilburne found the inspiration which led him to the career of revolutionary agitator.[6] These men went to their trial, not expecting justice, but seeking publicity. The pain and disgrace which befell them on the pillory were as nothing compared to the satisfaction of enacting such a part on such a stage before such an audience. Lilburne was quick and apt to better the instruction he received. While waiting in the Fleet after his trial of February 13, and before his punishment in April, he wrote a vivid account of his arraignment and conviction, *A Christian Mans Triall* (probably published in 1638; republished 1641, in which edition it is dated March 12, 1637/8). After his punishment, he was treated with savage cruelty, placed in solitary confinement in the Fleet, chained, prevented from communicating with his friends, and fed only by the connivance of other prisoners. In spite of all this, he yet contrived to get his story written and published. *A Worke of the Beast* appeared surreptitiously some time in 1638. *The Poore Mans Cry*, dated December 20,

---

[6] There is no biography of Lilburne. The best account is to be found in Pease's the *Leveller Movement*. For bibliography, see Peacock, *Notes and Queries, Seventh Series* (1888), 122, 162, 242, 342, 423, 502. The account of Lilburne's trial and suffering in *State Trials* is adapted from the pamphlets mentioned below.

1638, came out in the following year, as did *Come out of her My People*. *A Copy of a Letter . . . to the Wardens of the Fleet* is dated October 4, 1640. The Long Parliament gathered on November 3, and Lilburne was at once set free. He told the story again in 1646, in *A true relation of the materiall passages of Lieut. Col. John Lilburnes sufferings*.

A Worke of the Beast well illustrates the nature of the forces to be let loose in the Puritan Revolution. Lilburne on the pillory, making speeches and scattering pamphlets to the mob, was a portent rendered not less significant by the fact that prison walls could not stop the man from sending his story to circulate in print among the multitude. More clearly than in the cases of Prynne, Bastwick and Burton, his appeal to feelings of religion and justice is an expression of the common man's growing consciousness of interest and power in competitive society. Lilburne proclaims himself a Christian, an Englishman, a gentleman's son. Like many another such, he came to London to make his fortune in trade, and found the way made hard for him. Surely this was contrary to the laws of God and of nature. Surely the Bishops, as agents and symbols of vested authority, were to blame, and surely Lilburne possessed the native right to protect himself and to protest. With a sympathetic audience, with skill to act his part and to make his story known, with plausible formulas to make his case seem right, he represents a new power in society and a new problem for rulers.

II

NEW LIGHTS AND DIVINE RIGHT

ROBERT GREVILLE, LORD BROOKE

A Discourse opening the Nature of that Episcopacie, which is exercised in England.[7]

The insurrection against prelacy evidenced in the activities of Lilburne, Prynne, Burton and Bastwick, provoked Charles I to the series of acts which led to the Long Parliament, the overthrow of Strafford and Laud, the abolition of High Commission and Star Chamber, the introduction of the Root and Branch Bill for the abolition of episcopacy, and a general outcry for reform of church government. Reform of church government, however, carried with it the possibility of social revolution. Two fundamentally opposed conceptions of society were confusedly involved in the proposed abolition of prelacy. On the one hand, there was the ancient conception of society organized as a church with large powers over moral and intellectual life. On the other, there was a new way of regarding society as a secular nationalistic state, composed of individuals bound to civil obedience but otherwise free, a society in which the church should be reduced to the status of but one of an indefinite number of corporations with which the individual was at liberty to associate himself as he chose. The struggle began in the effort of the Puritan classes to wrest control of the established church from their opponents. Yet there were, from the beginning, abundant evidences of the coming forward of the more far-reaching question, whether the power of the church as a comprehensive social institution, vested with legal authority, should not definitely be reduced, if not destroyed. Only for a time did those who desired to restrict the church, in whatever degree, join forces with those who

[7] Vol. II, p. 35.

sought merely to possess themselves in some measure of the authority of the prelates. On every hand was beginning widespread, if confused, agitation on behalf of ideas and interests which could find scope only in a free secular society. Partisans of prelacy and of Presbyterianism at once found reason to accuse one another of weakening the defenses of the church against the forces of dissolution. Each could point to the imminence of schism or in other words revolution, in the activities of Independents, Anabaptists and Separatists of all sorts, while more discerning ears could hear in the clamor of the sects the cry of the common man for social justice.

The public discussion of the aims and principles of social reconstruction under the guise of reform of church government was undertaken by Bishop Joseph Hall in April, 1640, with advice from Laud himself. *Episcopacie by Divine Right Asserted*,[8] followed in January by *An Humble Remonstrance to the High Court of Parliament*, gave quasi-official expression to the plea that the overthrow of prelacy would be tantamount to the destruction of society itself. The counterclaim that, if society were to escape destruction, if in other words the church were to be saved from sects and schisms, prelacy must be replaced by Presbyterianism was put forth in a succession of replies to Hall. In January, 1641, Alexander Henderson published *The Unlawfulness and Danger of Limited Prelacie*, supported in October by Robert Baillie in *The Unlawfulness and Danger of Limited Episcopacie*. In February came the composite *Answer to . . . An Humble Remonstrance* by five Puritan preachers calling themselves Smectymnuus. *A Defence* by Hall, a *Vindication* by Smectymnuus, and a *Short Answer* by Hall followed one another in succession. Milton joined the attack on Hall with *Animadversions* (September), 1641, which provoked a *Modest Confutation* (January), 1642, to which Milton replied in an *Apology* (May).[9]

The pamphlets which passed at this juncture between pre-

[8] *Works*, Oxford 1863. See also Masson, *Milton*, II, 123-126, 214-218.
[9] Masson, *Milton*, II, 237-269.

lates and Presbyterians, except in the case of Milton, share certain significant characteristics. Both parties gave warning of the dangers of heresy and disunion. Both proceed by logic from Scripture and from what they took to be historical fact to the conclusion that God intended the church to be ruled by bishops or by presbyters, as the case might be. Neither is prepared to accept religious freedom, or to give any attention to the human problem presented by the unsatisfied needs and desires of those whom both agree to damn as heretics.

The injection of another point of view into the discussion, a point of view so alien in fact that it appears to have received little or no serious consideration, was the work of Milton. In *Lycidas*, written at the very moment when Laud had been persecuting Prynne, Burton, Bastwick and Lilburne, the poet had already shown his awareness of the spiritual needs of the populace and his indignation at the neglect of its responsibilities by the prelatical church. The intensity of his feeling on this point expressed itself again in the extraordinary flow of personal abuse which he directed against Hall in the pamphlets just mentioned. But his more significant contribution came in the three tracts, *Of Reformation* (June), 1641, *Of Prelatical Episcopacy* (July), and *The Reason of Church Government* (February), 1642. Milton wrote in general support of Smectymnuus, but Presbyterianism in his case was but a briefly held stage on the way to a poet's vision of a new society. Beyond Presbyterian discipline, Milton was looking to an ideal republic which would find strength in the limitation of its own powers and activities, while fostering those of a free, vigorous, self-reliant, intelligent citizenry. Thus it was his high distinction to propose that revolutionary unrest, instead of being put down as sin against the higher powers, be met by broad social policy, idealistically conceived.

The evidences of unrest were daily growing more abundant in the press. Unorganized as yet, there existed an important element in the Puritan population which was at least suspicious of any centralized control of or by the church. A confused but fermenting discontent was working among the middle classes, increasing rapidly in virulence and strength of numbers among the humbler and less prosperous. Its chief characteristic, seen through the eyes of religious and social prejudices, whether Anglican or Presbyterian, was the demand for toleration based upon the theory of a natural and inescapable liberty of conscience. The fear that anarchy might rise from such ideas in such quarters found expression in numerous satirical and abusive tracts such as *The Brownists Conventicle* of July, and *Religions Enemies* of November, 1641. A more serious effort to forfend chaos came from Thomas Edwards in *Reasons against the Independant Government of particular Congregations* (August), a work which had the distinction of being answered by a woman in Katherine Chidley's *Justification of the Independant Churches of Christ* (October).

The extreme revolutionary sects were for obvious reasons not quick to find utterance in the press, though their desires were no doubt expressed in the striking and well-written demand for religious liberty called *A New Petition of the Papists* (September) and in the almost identical *Humble Petition of the Brownists* (November) 1641.[10] What the left wing needed at the moment, however, was recognized leadership and organization. These were, we shall see, probably already in preparation at the hands of William Walwyn. In the meantime, encouragement and aggressive dogmatic assertion of liberty of conscience were being supplied by Henry Burton and John Goodwin. Both men were ministers to city congregations which favored Independent principles of church government somewhat after the New England model. That either foresaw the lengths to which the movement they were forwarding would go is doubtful, but at this juncture they boldly took up the plea of conscience against ecclesiastical regimentation. When Parliament adopted (May 4, 1641) a protestation of loyalty to the Protestant religion as "expressed in the doctrine

10 For the authorship of these tracts, see Appendix A, p. 126.

of the Church of England," Burton voiced his alarm in *The Protestation Protested* (July). In a sermon before Parliament on June 20, *Englands Bondage and Hope of Deliverance*, he entered a caveat on behalf of free conscience and independent government of congregations.

John Goodwin,[11] vicar of St. Stephen's, Coleman Street, was a younger and abler man than Burton. Educated at Cambridge, he had already distinguished himself by his boldness as a preacher and controversialist. A resourceful theologian and dialectician, he was fully persuaded that every problem under heaven could be settled by debate. To the cause of the revolutionary party, he brought the authority of his position as well as his great vigor and considerable ability. *The Saints Interest*, 1640, had brought upon him a choleric accusation of Socinianism from George Walker in *Socinianisme in the Fundamentall point of Justification*, 1641. Goodwin defended himself in *Impedit Ira*, 1641, and then unfolded at great length the doctrinal basis of his individualism in *Imputatio Fidei* (January 24), 1642. He rejected the extreme doctrine of predestination and urged that some degree of efficacy for salvation lay in the effort of individual reason to attain truth and of the individual will to pursue righteousness. He was consequently accused of Socinianism and Arminianism. His importance, however, is not to be found in his theology itself. The age required theological terms in which to express reasons for revolution as for nearly everything else in life. These Goodwin supplied, tirelessly, boldly and in abundance. His dialectic cast into approved intellectual molds the main currents of revolutionary thought, the growing determination of the revolutionary factions to overthrow tradition and authority in church and state, and to trust to the laws written by God in the heart of man.

Imputatio Fidei does not describe the outlook of the revolutionary sects of 1642 in terms readily intelligible to the modern reader. For that, one can best turn to Robert Greville, Lord

11 Thomas Jackson, *Life*, 1822.

Brooke, the cousin and adopted son of Fulke Greville, who had himself been the friend of Sidney and the favorite of Elizabeth. Brooke had early imbibed the humanistic idealism of the Renaissance. In 1640, his little treatise on *The Nature of Truth* summed up for his own satisfaction the Platonic doctrine of the One and the Many. Truth, he held, though diversely reflected throughout creation, is one, and the search for truth is a gathering up of the fragments which go to make the whole. Brooke became immediately involved in the great struggle as one of the most brilliant leaders on the Puritan side, and in November, 1641, came forward with *A Discourse opening the Nature of that Episcopacie which is exercised in England*. This pamphlet occupies a position in the development of revolutionary discussion which does not yield in importance to Milton's tracts of the same year. It is, in fact, much closer to the main current. The moment had come for the clergy and the religion of the clergy to be subjected to searching rational criticism. The clergy, it would be argued, owed their authority and their property solely to their ability to secure the obedience of the people to political powers which represented the oppressive weight of vested interest in society at large. To maintain themselves by maintaining such obedience, men would say, was, on the part of the clergy, the real purpose of uniformity and the underlying motive for persecution. Brooke's object in writing his pamphlet was to refute from this point of view the claims which Hall had put forth on the basis of Scripture and history. In his opening and closing chapters, however, he does something of larger significance. From the background of his Platonic idealism with its assertion of the immanence of the One in the Many, he takes the position that no act can be "indifferent," that every act is in the nature of things better or worse than another. Whether better or worse, reason alone can decide. The church, therefore, has authority to exact no obedience contrary to individual reason.

But Brooke is not content with rational criticism of specific

acts and policies of the bishops in question. The whole theory
of prelatism, betraying the law of reason and grasping for
worldly power, is for him as for Milton one with the cardinal
error of popery. He admits, perhaps merely in deference to
certain texts difficult otherwise to interpret, that the unpar-
donable sin may be found in the "Adamites," if there really
are any such people, or in the Familists, Antinomians and
Grindletonians,[12] unless they have been misrepresented. What,
however, were commonly called heresy and schism were in
his judgment merely evidence that truth or the broken
gleams of truth appeared diversely in the minds of all men.
Reason demanded that truth be sought and received in whatsoever form or fragment it appeared. A more striking application of such principles could hardly have been made. The
courtly idealism of the Elizabethan aristocrat is transformed
to the revolutionary doctrine of the law of reason, of the
inner light, of the natural necessity for toleration. Milton
recommended Brooke's pamphlet to the attention of Parliament itself: "Next to His last testament, who bequeathed love
and peace to his disciples, I cannot call to mind where I have
read or heard words more mild and peaceful" (*Areopagitica*).

Aside from the dramatic rebelliousness of Lilburne, the
discontent of the populace had expressed itself so far chiefly
in the form of separatist religious movements, almost universally despised, ridiculed and condemned. Milton himself had
not yet paid them serious attention. The chivalrous and idealistic Brooke now proposed that these people of the sects be
heard and that their claims be considered as freely and fairly
as those of any other members of society. Thus he did for
them what, for the most part, they were as yet unable to do
for themselves. He presented an intelligible statement of their
opinions and demands, and so enables us to discern the fea-
tures of the oncoming democratic movement. Approaching
the sects in a spirit similar to that of William Walwyn,
Brooke was led, like Walwyn, to believe that the spiritual

[12] Concerning these sects see below, pp. 34-37, 43.

brotherhood of man was to be realized not in religious uniformity but in civil society. He, too, felt the appeal of those
notions of the sects which, stripped of extravagance, spoke to
him of light and love, of truth shining in all men's breasts and
uniting them by reason and discourse one with another.

III

THE LAW OF NATURE

[HENRY PARKER]

Observations upon some of his Majesties late Answers and Expresses [13]

The close of 1641 was marked by the rapid approach of war. On the first of November, news reached London of the Irish rebellion. The Grand Remonstrance quickly followed. Brooke's *Episcopacie* appeared, and in December the mob was shouting "No bishops" at the doors of Parliament. In February, prelates were debarred from the House of Lords. At the same time, the quarrel over episcopacy was widening to an open breach between Parliament and the king. On the fourth of January, Charles made his futile attempt upon the five members, and a few days later set out for the north. In March, Parliament voted to put the kingdom in a posture of defense. In April, Sir John Hotham denied the royal summons to surrender Hull. War began, and moved on to the Battle of Edgehill at the end of October. The king marched upon London as far as Turnham Green, and then settled at Oxford for the winter.

The inconclusiveness of these operations and the confused efforts for peace which attended them reflected the indecision of men's minds. The question was no longer whether the church should be ruled by bishops, but whether Parliament and people might rightfully resist the crown by force of arms. In the confusion of loyalties and judgments provoked by that question, all parties rushed into print. Men of opposing convictions might agree that decision rested with God, whose will was to be found in some absolute rule revealed in his word. They might deplore the intrusion of individual human opinion into the settlement of such questions. They might particularly

[13] Vol. II, p. 165.

deplore the publication of conflicting opinions. Yet the practical exigency which forced itself upon all contenders was the need for such support as might be secured by appeal to the public through the press. Hence the messages and addresses that came from Charles in the course of his controversy with Parliament were immediately put into print, and were directly attended by an outpouring of pamphlets representing all shades of feeling and judgment on the opposition of the divine right of revolution to the divine right of established interests.

The defenders of established interests had the initial advantage of being able to summon sentiment, loyalty and the appearance of legality to their aid. The proponents of revolution had to discover some no less moving appeal. The character which that was to take and to keep was decisively indicated by Henry Parker. Born in 1604, educated at Oxford, called to the bar at Lincoln's Inn in the crucial year 1637, Parker seems to have derived his ideas of the law of nature and the social contract from Fortescue and Hooker. He now brought them to the support of the parliamentary cause. In *The Case of Shipmony*, 1640, he had asserted that "the supreme of all humane lawes is *salus populi*" and that "that iron law which wee call necessity itselfe is but subservient to this law; for rather than a Nation shall perish, anything shall be held necessary, and legal by necessity." In 1641, he had applied this principle to the defense of Parliament and people against episcopal domination in *A Discourse concerning Puritans* (January), and in *The True Grounds of Ecclesiasticall Regiment* (November). Then, in 1642, he turned it against the king himself in *Some Few Observations upon his Majesties late Answer* (May 21), promptly expanded into *Observations upon some of his Majesties late Answers and Expresses* (July 2; second edition 1642). He reiterated his points briefly in *A Petition humbly desired to be presented to his Majestie* (July 17), and *The Danger to England observed upon its deserting Parliament* (July 28).

Parker opposed royalism with the claim that "Power is originally inherent in the people." In support of this position, he brought forward a statement of the myth and doctrine of the social contract. Man's first law was the natural law that God wrote in the human breast, but after the fall of Adam men grew so depraved that this was no longer enough to preserve them from one another. Hence they were led to the social contract, by which they agreed to set up and obey a magistrate who should in turn agree to rule over them solely for their protection. When, however, violating his agreement, the magistrate seeks the destruction of the people, then "the iron law of necessity" serves to protect his subjects through Parliament, of which they are the "essence." The notion that this necessity might function through channels other than Parliament does not seem to have occurred to Parker.

The defense of Parliament was also presently undertaken by William Prynne in a series of tremendous tracts which even at the time were significant rather of the extent of their author's prestige than for anything they contained. Prynne's method as a pamphleteer was directly contrary to Parker's. The latter attempted to make a candid and temperate appeal to reason in language which could readily be understood. Prynne knew himself assured of a hearing because of his learning, his zeal and his sufferings. He laid down his position with fierce dogmatism and inundated disagreement with uncritical erudition, stuffing hundreds of pages with citations from law, history, Scripture and the fathers, heaped together in fantastic confusion. Few if any readers could have followed Prynne with understanding. But one thing was clear in what he wrote, the unquestioning assertion of parliamentary supremacy, and many an earnest if simple mind must have been persuaded that truth must surely lie where, in so good a cause, appeared so much zeal and learning. Hence the contemporary importance of those huge heaps of printed pages which Prynne threw off in *A Soveraign Antidote* (August 18), 1642; *A Revindication of the Anoynting and Priviledges of faithfull*

Subjects (January 6), 1643; *The Treachery and Disloyalty of Papists to their Soveraignes* (March 16); and *The Soveraigne Power of Parliaments* (three parts in continuation of the preceding pamphlet, April 15, June 23, August 28).

Judged by the attention it received in the press, Parker's *Observations* was far more important than all of Prynne's outpourings. The adroit and plausible application to the crisis of 1642 of the well-known theory of the social contract became the starting-point of momentous discussion. Not the least important effect of Parker's tract was to be its influence on John Lilburne. But Lilburne for the time being was at the war, and the immediate effect was to call forth a stream of Royalist replies and parliamentary rejoinders, which continued until in the ensuing year Parliament attempted to stem the tide by censorship of the press.[14] Within a week of publication, *Observations* seems to have been visited with the *Animadversions* of an Oxford pen. During the ensuing year, hardly a week went by without the appearance of something in print dealing directly with Parker's argument or the discussion it had provoked. Sir John Spelman testified that no book had done so much to entangle and intoxicate the vulgar. As a result of such licentious publications, he said, Londoners had become like the citizens of Abdera, who, "hearing a strange tragedy full of seditious designes, they were all strucken into such a fit of Phrensie, That for many dayes after, they did nothing but

[14] *Animadversions upon those Notes which the late Observator hath published* (July 9), 1642, (Thomason adds "Oxon."). *An Answer or necessary Animadversions upon some late Impostumate Observations* (August 3). Parker replied to the former in *Animadversions Animadverted* (August 6). Among other direct attacks on Parker were: William Ball, *A Caveat for Subjects* (September 19); Sir John Spelman *View of a Printed Book* (January 26), 1643; *Christus Dei* (March 7); *A Review of the Observations* (April 15); *An Examination of the Observations* (August 14); John Bramhall, *The Serpent Salve*. Parker again replied to his opponents in *The Contra-Replicant* (January 31), and still again in *Jus Populi* (October 16), 1644. With John Sadler and Thomas May he was later entrusted by Parliament with the publication of the king's papers captured at Naseby, *The Kings Cabinet opened* (June 14), 1645. The fullest statement of the formal argument for the law of nature and the social contract in support of Parliament came finally not from Parker but from Samuel Rutherford in the four hundred and sixty-six pages of *Lex, Rex: The Law and the Prince* (October 7), 1644.

act the same Tragedy, with furious gestures in their streets." [15]

Of all the Royalist tracts provoked by Parker, two deserve particular notice. These were Ferne's *Resolving of Conscience*,[16] 1642, and Sir Dudley Digges's *Answer to a Printed Book* (November 20), expanded later into *The Unlawfulnesse of Subjects taking up Armes* (January 15), 1644. Rather in sorrow than in anger, Ferne presented the plea that the people should not resist their natural ruler, since resistance could in no circumstance be approved by conscience. Digges argued more realistically that to dissolve the social contract by rebellion against the appointed sovereign was not to defend but to destroy the public safety. "When every man exercises his natural freedom, no man is free." Ferne and Digges thus early advanced the two aspects, sentimental and rational, of the position which the supporters of monarchy were eventually to exploit with so much success. Ferne's appeal for loyalty to the king as father of the people began to prepare the way for *Eikon Basilike* (February 9), 1649, and for Filmer's *Anarchy of a Limited or Mixed Monarchy* (April 19), 1648, and his well-known *Patriarcha* (1680). Digges's

[15] *View of a Printed Book.*

[16] *The Resolving of Conscience, Upon this Question, Whether upon such a Supposition or Case, as is now usually made (The King will not discharge his trust, but is bent or seduced to subvert Religion, Laws, and Liberties) Subjects may take Arms and resist?* . . . Cambridge, 1642. There is a copy of the second edition in the McAlpin Collection, "Printed at *Cambridge*, and reprinted at *London*, 1642." This pamphlet probably appeared not later than October, since John Goodwin in *Anti-Cavalierisme*, October 21, though without specific mention of the work, seems clearly to be refuting its arguments. Charles Herle published *An Answer to Misled Doctor Fearne* of which the Thomason Collection has a copy dated November 29, 1642, though this is nowhere indicated in the Thomason Catalogue (see volume press-marked E 244). An enlarged edition appeared as *A Fuller Answer* (December 29), 1642. William Bridge answered Ferne in *The Wounded Conscience cured* (February 11), 1643, which was printed by order of the House of Commons. Still another reply appeared as *Scripture and Reason pleaded for Defensive Armes . . . Published by diverse . . . Divines* and also printed (April 14), 1643, with Parliamentary sanction. Ferne answered his critics in *Conscience Satisfied* (April 18), which elicited another *Answer* from Herle (May 17), and *The Truth of the Times Vindicated* from Bridge (July 24). In *A Reply unto severall Treatises pleading for the Armes now taken up by Subjects* (November 1), Ferne gave particular attention to the ministerial *Scripture and Reason.*

view of the social contract anticipated that of Hobbes's *Leviathan*, 1651.

The pamphlets which thus attended the outbreak of the civil war were significant not alone for their bearing on the development of political theory. They also played an important part in the development of public consciousness, of the function and theory of public opinion. The writers so far mentioned were, to be sure, attempting to establish an absolute right, whether of king or Parliament, grounded upon an absolute law of God and nature. The weakness common to them all was that their absolute could in practice be made to prevail, only if enough people could be persuaded to believe it absolute or be forcibly prevented from thinking and persuading others to think otherwise. To minds more shrewd or less inclosed in their own logic, this fact was becoming more and more apparent. Public opinion and the control of public opinion were rapidly becoming factors of more practical importance than any law written in Scripture or on the tables of the breast. To many earnest souls, this was a condition alarming in the extreme, and pamphlets began to deplore the publication of pamphlets. It would seem that even Henry Parker shared this concern, and put his pen at the service of the Stationers' Company in the effort to secure an ordinance from Parliament for putting a check upon the freedom of the press.[17] The confusion of minds on this point was also well exemplified by the ministerial authors of *Scripture and Reason Pleaded*, who expressed the horror commonly felt that men should not only fight and kill but also argue and print in these disputes. " 'Tis a bitter Controversie that our poore sinfull Nation is fallen upon, wherein not onely Armes are ingaged against Armes, but Bookes written against Bookes, and Conscience pretended against Conscience."

Philip Hunton, though hardly less confused, was in one respect able to attain a more realistic view of the situation.

---

[17] See below, p. 47.

In his *Treatise of Monarchie* (May 24), 1643,[18] he labors like others to unriddle the predicament by defining an absolute basis for government. Finding himself unable, however, to excogitate a theoretical supremacy for either king or Parliament when the two clashed, he concluded more candidly than most writers that "in this case, which is beyond the Government, the Appeal must be to the Community, as if there were no Government; and as by evidence mens Consciences are convinced, they are bound to give their utmost assistance." This admission, however pertinent, of course worked havoc to all customary political theories, including Hunton's own. Ferne exclaimed in derision, "Here is good stuffe," and pointed out that such appeal to the community "was never given as a Rule before." Hunton in reply again insisted on the "seminall" power of the people. Filmer, early in the series of pamphlets in which he did so much to persuade the community that it had no right to expect persuasion, easily exposed the logical difficulty of Hunton's preposterous but apposite discovery that the approval of the community might be practically indispensable to the exercise of authority over it.

[18] Another edition 1680, 1689; reprinted in the "Harleian Miscellany," VI. See Ferne *A Reply Unto Severall Treatises* (November 1), 1643, Hunton *Vindication of the Treatise of Monarchy* (March 26), 1644, Filmer *The Anarchy of a Limited or Mixed Monarchy* (April 19), 1648.

IV

THE CALL FOR POPULAR RESISTANCE

JOHN GOODWIN

Anti-Cavalierisme [19]

The appeal to the community, which Hunton held up as at least a theoretical contingency, was rapidly becoming a fact. The confusion of conflict between crown and Parliament gave opportunity for the rise of men skilled in the art of evoking and manipulating opinion. Such men were soon to find that they could exercise influence which, unacknowledged and discountenanced as it was, might yet prove sufficient to put awry the best laid schemes of kings and parliamentary majorities. William Walwyn was actively if quietly at work among despised sectaries such as would presently fill up Cromwell's army. Meanwhile, the man rising most conspicuously as a leader of public opinion was John Goodwin. After the controversy which had given occasion to *Imputatio Fidei*, the vicar of St. Stephen's in Coleman Street had been consolidating on Independent lines a compact, earnest congregation of vigorous adherents. He now published a tract called *Anti-Cavalierisme* (October 21), 1642, followed directly by another in the same vein called *The Butchers Blessing* (November 4; the two appeared together in a second edition in 1643). These preachments were not controversial pamphlets written to swell the stream of polemic started by Parker. They were inflammatory sermons, intended to rouse the city on the occasion of the Battle of Edgehill and the march of Charles to Turnham Green. Goodwin wholeheartedly accepted the view of the state advanced by Parker. Parliament represented the people, and the safety of the people was menaced by the butcherly brood

[19] Vol. II, p. 215.

THE SUCKLINGTON FACTION: OR (SUCKLINGS) ROARING BOYES

From a broadside in the Thomason Collection in the British Museum [669 f 4 (17)], 1641.

who had seduced the king from his obligation under the contract. Resistance was justified, nay imposed, by the law written by God in the heart and supported by Scripture. But Goodwin handles these arguments with a difference. He does not protract the logomachy of Parker and Ferne. He seeks to terminate discussion, hesitation and confusion by precipitating action, and he uses all the resources of the popular preacher to that end. Abandoning abstractions, he lays hold of language calculated to put the men of his day in the mood to fight. He has, of course, to marshal controverted biblical texts at greater length than the modern reader will entirely relish, but he does so less to find premises for unsteady syllogisms than moving images or at least inciting principles of conduct. He brings to his purpose a power of expression greater than that of any writer of the moment except Milton, who for some reason took no part in the present debate. His sentences are the rolling periods of seventeenth-century imprecation, but they are eloquent and not turgid. Above all, Goodwin overcame brilliantly one of the major stylistic difficulties of his time and profession by incorporating biblical images alive into his discourse instead of depositing them as so much dead matter upon his page.

We have in *Anti-Cavalierisme*, therefore, rather than in any of the other works which have just been discussed, the clearest expression of the revolutionary aspect of the controversy over the social contract. Goodwin's provocative preaching probably carried further than we can now venture to say. Among all the preachers in London, his was the most active mind, the boldest voice and the readiest pen, and he probably deserved the sobriquet bestowed upon him by Thomas Edwards of "Great Red Dragon of Coleman Street." For the present, he lent his aid to Parliament. In so doing, however, he was drawing closer the lines of a compact and influential group of men in the city of whom he was to be the acknowledged voice and leader. Thus he organized a body of opinion, fully articulate and too powerful to be summarily denied, ready to support first the Independent minority in the Westminster Assembly, and then, in alliance with the Levellers, Cromwell and the Army against Parliament itself. In 1649 he would be ready to justify Pride's Purge, and by anticipation the execution of Charles, precisely upon the grounds of his defense of Parliament in 1642.[20]

[20] *Anti-Cavalierisme* was attacked by Griffith Williams in *Vindiciae Regum* (February 1), 1643, to which Goodwin replied in *Os Ossorianum or a Bone for a Bishop to pick* (April 11). In justifying resistance to the king's agents, Goodwin admitted that the actual life of the king was sacred and not to be assailed. In his *Right and Might* of 1649 this distinction could no longer be maintained. Sir Francis Nethersole taxes Goodwin with time-serving on this score in ʽΟ ᾽αυτο-κατάκριτος, *The Self-Condemned* (January 8), 1649. Goodwin defended himself in ʽΟ κριτὴς τῆς ᾽αδικίας, *The Unrighteous Judge* (January 25), but was twitted again on the same point by Walwyn's friend, Henry Brooke, in *The Charity of Churchmen* (May 28).

V

THE PLEA FOR TOLERANCE

[WILLIAM WALWYN]

The Power of Love [21]

Most men in 1642 expected that, if Parliament succeeded in its efforts against the crown and the prelates, reformation of the church would swiftly be effected on Presbyterian lines. Presbyterianism was commonly understood to be a highly organized system by which individual conduct in all phases of life would be brought under strict control by the parish clergy. Even Milton took, momentarily, a sanguine view of the possibilities of such discipline. "First constitute that which is right, and of itself it will discover and rectify that which swerves, and easily remedy the pretended fear of having a pope in every parish, unless we call the zealous and meek censure of the church a popedom." [22] Nevertheless, resistance to the imposition of such censure was to prove no less determined, and in its results no less important, than resistance to royal absolutism. This had already been foreshadowed by Lord Brooke. It grew ominous in the rise of John Goodwin. It now began to receive reasoned statement in two anonymous tracts which probably came from the hand of William Walwyn, *Some Considerations tending to the undeceiving those, whose judgements are misinformed* (November 10), 1642, and *The Power of Love* (September 19), 1643.

Goodwin was not the man to look forward hopefully to the enforcement of Presbyterian discipline. His active mind had already carried him far from strict Calvinism, and would carry him yet further. At the same time, he was the mouthpiece of prosperous tradesmen sufficiently conscious of their interest

[21] Vol. II, p. 271. [22] *Of Reformation.*

to fear the interference of the church in their affairs. As a successful preacher, he did not himself wish to be limited in his opportunities either for service or for the tangible rewards of service. He did not wish to be confined either by the boundaries of a parish or by the dictates of a synod, composed, it might be, of competitors for popular favor. At any rate, the entrance of Goodwin into the arena of public discussion marked the rise in the church of a party which favored an Independent or Congregational form of church government after the general model of New England. One must clearly note, in order to understand what followed, that this was not a movement consciously directed against the historic church but a movement within the church against centralized government and the geographical restriction of the parish. What the Independents desired was the freedom of churches gathered under regular ministers in congregations.[23] They did not set out to seek freedom for individuals to be of any or of no religion, or for groups outside the church to form religious societies upon whatsoever doctrinal basis they chose. The logic of events drove them in the direction of a larger freedom than they could approve, and, when the time came, they retreated willingly to the Cromwellian compromise, which tolerated only such quiet, respectable, law-abiding groups as would support the existing government.

Outside the church, outside the recognized Independent

[23] Cf. W. A. Shaw, *History of the English Church*, II, 34-36: "The basis of the movement towards freedom of thought and toleration . . . was secular, and so far from championing it in whole or in essence, the Independents of the first period of the Civil War, the clerical Independents, used it only as a weapon in their faction fight against a presbytery which would have quickly extinguished them. One's sympathies can hardly go with either, for the perception grows that the contribution of the Dissenting Brethren to the great cause of ecclesiastical and intellectual freedom was accidental. It was only when the initiative passed back to the laity, when the weary wranglings of the Assembly gave place to the agitations in the New Model, that a true conception of liberty of conscience reëmerged." The only modification to be made in Shaw's very just statement of the matter is that the initiative was taken by the laity in the persons of Walwyn and Lilburne before the New Model had got under way, and that these men, especially the former, were influenced in an important if peculiar way by the sects.

congregations such as Goodwin's in Coleman Street and Burton's in Friday Street, to some extent but not wholly outside the social ranks from which the Independents at first drew their strength, were the true sects.[24] The sectarian movement had sprung up in the course of the English Reformation, and led to the emergence at the opening of the century of various groups called by such names as Brownists, Barrowists, Separatists, Anabaptists, Familists and the like. The common distinctive characteristic of all the sects was refusal to recognize the historic church. They sought to withdraw from the church, and so from service to the state with which it was involved. They denied membership to those unconverted to their own views and moral practices. The doctrinal differences of the several sects do not concern us here. Though upon the crucial question of free will and predestination they, like the church itself, were not at one, they were in general Antinomian in tendency and looked rather to Luther and the German and Dutch mystics than to Calvin.

Such were the characteristics of the sects as religious bodies. In the disintegration of medieval popular culture, they provided some precarious outlet for the groping aspirations of the common people after a better life. As the old order dissolved, they provided both spiritual ideals and a pattern of expression for the popular mind. Hence came that seemingly prodigious eruption of heresies and sects in 1640, when restraints were suddenly released. To the excited apprehension of the secure and respectable classes, every novel opinion about anything in heaven or earth, when it came from the uneducated and the unpossessed, was, of course, a heresy. Every heresy was thought to be represented by a sect, and every sect was feared as a conspiracy against all law and morality. Satan had broken loose, breathing error into vulgar breasts. Every base mechanic was ready to mount a tub, gather a conventicle, and seek the overthrow of society. The truth was that these

---

[24] Burrage, *Early English Dissenters*; R. M. Jones, *Spiritual Reformers in the Sixteenth and Seventeenth Centuries*. Masson's list of sects (*Milton* III, 136-160) may be used with caution.

manifestations of spiritual turmoil in the lower classes sprang
in part from genuine religious feeling, from naïve mysticism,
from semiliterate yearning for poetic expression. Partly they
were ill-directed, sometimes knavish, attempts to escape from
the harness of customary morality. Partly they were the
clumsy but honest gestures of the vulgar after freedom and
social justice. That the tub preachers and the excitement they
aroused were a menace to the maintenance of order, especially
to the authority of the clergy, there can be no question. They
met, therefore, with violent condemnation from prelatist and
Presbyterian alike, and at best with deprecation from the Independents.[25] At the same time, each party of the right in
turn accused its opponents on the left of seeking to open a
door that would let loose an Egyptian plague of heresies and
schisms. Assaults on the sects were animated, one need hardly
say, by prejudice, the sense of vested interest, clerical jealousy,
prurience and vulgar sensationalism, as well as by zealous conviction of righteousness, true piety, and honest fear of
disorder.

[25] Typical of the kind of attack that emanated first from prelatist and then
from Presbyterian sources were the following pamphlets of 1641: *A Swarme of
Sectaries and Schismatiques, wherein is discovered the strange preaching
(or prating) of Coblers, Tinkers . . . and Chymney Sweepers* (June) by John
Taylor; *The Brownists Conventicle: or an assemble of Brownists, Separatists,
and Non-Conformists, as they met together at a private house to heere a Sermon
of a brother of theirs neere Algate, being a learned Felt-maker* (July) [has an
indecent woodcut satirizing the sectaries, which may have appeared earlier, and
which reappeared frequently in later tracts of similar nature]; *A Discoverie of
Six Women Preachers. . . . With a relation of their names, manners, life and
doctrine* (August); *A Discovery of 29 Sects here in London* (September);
*Description of the Sect called the Family of Love, with their place of residence.
Discovered by Susannah Snow* [a young woman who professes to have been
temporarily seduced by this sect at the cost of her innocence] (October); *A
Curb for Sectaries and bold Propheciers, By which Richard Farnham the
Weaver, James Hunt the Farmer, M. Greene the Felt-maker, and all other the
like bold Propheciers and Sect Leaders may be bridled* (November); *Religions
Enemies. With a brief and ingenious Relation, as by Anabaptists, Brownists,
Papists, Familiarists, Atheists, and Foolists, sawcily presuming to tosse Religion
in a Blanquet* (November); *The Discovery of a Swarme of Separatists, or a
Leathersellers Sermon* (December 19); *New Preachers, new. Greene the felt-
maker, Spencer the horse-rubber, Quartermine the brewers clarke* (December
19); *A Tale in a Tub; or, A Tub Lecture, as it was delivered by My-heele
Mendsoale, an Inspired Brownist, in a meeting-house near Bedlam* (December 21).

The sects were vulnerable enough, but they had their elements of nobility. There were germs in them which a discerning mind could perceive and hope to make grow into something better than the extravagances of tub preachers. Among the sects, as among few prelatists, Presbyterians or Independents, was to be found that sense of common need which sometimes makes men sink themselves in joint action for the common good. Notions of freedom, equality and brotherhood ran through the Antinomian mysticism. Justification, as they expressed it, was free to all. Men were not some damned and some elect, but all alike in their title to salvation. They were not bound by divine decree to suffer inexpressible punishment for ineluctable sin, but free to live good lives, to be happy as brothers in the equal expectation of grace. If they failed to obtain happiness, the reason was not the primal defect of human nature but the remediable defect of laws and institutions which had been corrupted in process of time by ignorance and by the selfishness which plays upon and breeds ignorance. On the other hand, if men would be happy, they must free themselves from distrust; they must begin at once to live lovingly like brothers, fearing only ignorance and following only reason.

We are not to suppose that every tub preacher clearly entertained such thoughts. Yet there was one man at least, to whom, at about this time, such conceptions did emerge as a kind of rational goal towards which the enthusiasms of the sects might be led by good-tempered persuasion and appeal to common sense. This man was William Walwyn, and the point of view which was so singularly his received characteristic expression in *Some Considerations* and *The Power of Love*.[26]

[26] Pease (*The Leveller Movement*, 242-254), who gives the best account of Walwyn, finds his personality baffling and his real influence impossible to estimate, though "easier underestimated than overestimated." Pease, whose positive inferences are always sound and useful, fails, nevertheless, in this instance to take sufficient account of the acknowledged influence on Walwyn of Montaigne, and to identify a number of important anonymous tracts of Walwyn. For Masson's derogatory remark concerning Walwyn (*Milton*, IV,

William Walwyn, almost completely forgotten as he has
been, was one of the most remarkable men of his time. Sprung
from yeoman stock in Worcestershire, the grandson of a bishop, he was in 1640 about forty years old, a member of the
Merchant Adventurers and master of a comfortable fortune
acquired in trade. He had lived some fifteen years in the parish
of St. James, Garlick Hill, where he had been active in the
reform of the parish church and then of the affairs of the ward.
Before July, 1645, he moved to Moorfields, where he had a
garden and a library in which he occasionally entertained his
friends. He was devoted to his wife, who bore him twenty
children and whose opinions he thought worthy of quoting
at some length in one of his pamphlets.[27] He was destined to
play a large part in the Leveller movement, and no man of the
time reveals more clearly some of the elusive intellectual
origins of democratic radicalism. Walwyn was averse to publicity for himself and preferred to work by personal intercourse and discussion. He published little, and that for the
most part anonymously. The pamphlets he did put forth are
peculiarly incisive statements of a point of view held with
great tenacity.

Early in his career, Walwyn says, he was convinced by "that
part of doctrine [called then, Antinomian] of free justification by Christ alone; and so my heart was at much more ease
and freedom than others." [28] Liberated from the entangle-
ments to which "Sermons and Doctrines mixt of Law and
Gospel do subject distressed consciences," he could say "I am
one that do truely and heartily love all mankind, it being the
unfeigned desire of my soul, that all men might be saved,
and come to the knowledge of the truth." [29] Though he knew
no language but English, and never travelled out of England,
he was nevertheless a habitual reader of "humane authors,"
"the most of my recreation being a good Book, or an honest
and discoursing friend." [30] The testimony of enemies confirms

---

45), there is no ground whatever. For the identification of Walwyn's authorship
of the anonymous tracts attributed to him in these pages, see Appendix A.
  [27] *Just Defence.*   [28] *Just Defence,* 8.   [29] *Whisper,* 2.
  [30] *Just Defence,* 9, *Fountain,* 22.

this statement by personal details intended to seem discreditable. They show Walwyn moving about among all sorts of
people, asking embarrassing questions with disarming genial-
ity, entrapping the unwary into puzzling conversations on
delicate points of religion, luring serious young men to his
home and there in his library offering them dubious and pagan
books.[31] Walwyn in self-defense gives an account of his reading (*Just Defence*, 9). The Bible comes first, but with the
qualification that he is constrained by no power other than
his own understanding of the text to believe it the word of
God. Then come various works of Protestant divinity, Hooker,
Hall, Perkins and Downham. In Hall, he read the "meditations, and vowes, and his heaven upon earth," works in which
the so-called English Seneca gave a kind of Anglican version
of Stoicism. In Hooker, it was "those peeces annexed to . . .
Ecclesiasticall Polity," by which was probably meant the
strictures of Hooker on the Calvinism of Travers and other
opponents. But in addition to these works, Walwyn was in the
habit of "using *Seneca, Plutarchs Lives*, and *Charon of humane
wisdom*,[32] as things of recreation, wherein I was both pleased
and profited." Against Cicero, whose orations he had seen but
not read, he felt a certain prejudice, "esteeming him a verball
and vain-glorious writer"; and Plutarch's *Morals* he found
tedious. Both Walwyn and his friend, Dr. Henry Brooke, were
at pains to protest that, though the former may have pulled
Lucian down from the shelves, he did not say to the young man
to whom he recommended the book, "Here is more wit in this
then in all the Bible." Nevertheless he admits that "*Lucian*
for his good ends, in discovering the vanity of things in worldly esteem, I like very well." [33] But perhaps the most striking
name to find on Walwyn's list of authors is Montaigne. "I
blush not to say I have long been accustomed to read *Mon-
taignes Essaies*." Surely no one else in that age would have

[31] Kiffen and others, *Walwins Wiles*.

[32] Pierre Charron, *Traité de la sagesse*, 1601, English translation by Samson
Lennard, published in 1612.

[33] *Walwins Wiles*, 9; *Just Defence*, 9; Brooke, *Charity of Churchmen*, 4.

ventured to make the use that this man did of that great, but
by no means godly, book. A prisoner in the Tower, having
to defend himself against a charge of irreligion, Walwyn
quotes several times at some length from the *Essays*, particularly from *Of the Cannibals*, and he recommends the charity
of Montaigne for the emulation of his critics, the Independent
and Baptist preachers. Some years before in *The Power of
Love*, he had opened what purported to be a Familist haran-
gue with a discussion of the state of nature reminiscent of that
passage of the same essay on cannibals which had also engaged
the fancy of Shakespeare.

The account of Walwyn's reading goes far to illuminate
for us what we know of his career, and to suggest one source
of Leveller enthusiasm. The man had absorbed the tolerant
skepticism of Renaissance humanism toward religious dogma.
He had become deeply imbued with Montaigne's Socratic
curiosity concerning human nature. He had, moreover, effected
for himself that transposition of Christian myth into romantic
revolutionary images which held so much of significance for
the future. The will of God was the law of nature, discover-
able by reason. The state of innocence was the state of nature,
as Montaigne's cannibal island so engagingly hinted. The fall
of man, being very largely the result of ignorance, was re-
trievable. Not man but men were depraved. Society was
in large measure the encumbrance, the "many inventions,"
imposed upon man by his own folly and selfishness. Redemption was to be found in the recovery of the natural state by
love and reason. Moved by such ideas, Walwyn took to no
sect, nor did he trouble to break communion with the church.
For twenty years before the Long Parliament, he remained
"a serious and studious reader and observer of things necessary." He investigated "all the severall doctrines and waies of
worship that are extant." He undertook to persuade other
men to examine in the same spirit their own and others' beliefs,
and to inquire always into the hidden motives of persecution.
When the Revolution came, he took upon himself the rôle of

Samaritan, defending from persecution not himself but others, not his own religion but that of Separatist and Independent.

Precisely what Walwyn owed to the ideas of the sects is impossible to say. He may, perhaps, have derived from them that Antinomian doctrine of free justification which he found productive of so much peace and freedom of mind. But if he accepted the Antinomianism of the sects, it was in no doctrinaire spirit, and it was without the mysticism in which the doctrine was by them involved: "I abandon all niceties and useless things: my manner is in all disputes or reasoning and discourses, to inquire what is the use." "For the publike Liberties," says Brooke, "he hath not only appeared, but rescued most of them out of a heap of contrary Doctrines, and Politick concealments." From Montaigne and other "humane authors," he could have derived the ideal of society as a union of men with equal rights to well-being, working together peacefully in rational pursuit of the common good. What he found "useful" in the sects was something essentially the same. He thought he found in them men who desired to live at peace with their fellows, willing to be persuaded by reason, and disinclined to impose their own opinions by force upon others. They were common men in humble stations for the most part, and therefore devoid of material interests that could be secured by religious intolerance.

The point of view thus peculiarly characteristic of Walwyn was expressed in 1642 in an anonymous tract of sixteen pages, called *Some Considerations Tending to the undeceiving those, whose judgements are misinformed by Politique Protestations, Declarations, &c. Being a necessary discourse for the present times, concerning the unseasonable difference between the Protestant and the Puritan* (November 10). A still more striking expression of the same attitude appeared in *The Power of Love* (September 19), during the ensuing year. *Some Considerations* is a warning to the supporters of Parliament not to permit dissension to be sown among them by accusations leveled against the sects. Not that the author is himself a sectary, but that he counts all good men his friends. The sectaries are friends to Parliament, religion, liberty and the law. Those who seek to persecute them serve their own selfish ends under cover of zeal for religion. They use words to set men quarreling over shadows, and so make slaves of them, breeding clergymen in the university for this very purpose. All who would serve the public good must therefore stand together, and not permit themselves to be deceived by accusations of heresy directed by known enemies against known friends of the common cause. "We have all need one of another."

The Power of Love, at first glance, as the opening sentence of the Epistle dares to suggest, purports to be a discourse by some member of the Family of Love. Upon closer view, it proves to be nothing of the sort. Familist preachers were not in the habit of reading Montaigne, or of composing persuasive pleas for tolerance in language which is both moving and easily understood. By boldly pretending to speak as a Familist, the writer aims to seize the attention of readers who ignorantly regard Familism with horror. He then puts before them in appealing and intelligible form the useful, rational and admirable element in this harmless and abused sect. This rational and politic rather than sectarian or even religious attitude points clearly to Walwyn, and the skill, the imaginative power, with which it is sustained, is not again to be met until we come to that recantation which Walwyn put into the mouth of Thomas Edwards himself.[34] *The Power of Love* does, however, show genuine familiarity with Familist doctrine. Moreover, one of the distinguishing marks of Walwyn's writing is the constant recurrence of the plea, made with peculiar intensity, for the spirit of love as the only ground for a flourishing and happy state. It is not unlikely, therefore, that among the sects the Family of Love particularly attracted him and influenced his thinking.

The Family of Love was a sect originated in Holland about

[34] *Prediction*; see below, p. 110.

1541, by Hendrik Niclaes.[35] Ten years later Niclaes seems to have spent some time in England, and about 1575 many of his works appeared in English translation. A sect of English Familists seems to have got itself established by 1580, when Elizabeth made proclamation against them. Notwithstanding persecution, they continued to hold together, becoming a special object of horror at the outbreak of the Revolution because of their alleged immorality. John Hetherington, a box-maker, was forced to abjure Familist doctrines at Paul's Cross in 1627, and there is evidence of the existence of other Familists about the same time at Grindleton in Yorkshire.[36] John Everard, the translator of various works of German mystics, was charged before High Commission in 1636 with Familism, Antinomianism and Socinianism. John Eaton published a work of Familist or Antinomian edification in 1642, called *Honey-Combe of Free Justification*. Giles Randall, from 1643 to 1650, became notorious as a preacher of similar heresies and as in some fashion the translator (or the editor of Everard's translations) of the German mystics. Beginning in 1646, many of the translated works of Niclaes himself were reprinted by Giles Calvert, well known as the publisher of all sorts of sectarian and heretical literature. In the confusion of the Revolution, the Familists are lost to sight, while their place is taken by sects like the Seekers, the General Baptists, the Ranters and the Quakers. Among all these groups, Anti-

[35] F. Nippold, *Heinrich Niclaes und das Haus der Liebe* in *Zeitschrift für die historische Theologie*, xxxii (1862). Largely based upon this is the account in Barclay's *Inner Life of the Religious Societies of the Commonwealth*, 25-35; and in Burrage's *Early English Dissenters*, 209-214. The article on Henry Nicholas in the *Dictionary of National Biography* has a useful bibliography. R. M. Jones' *Spiritual Reformers* gives details concerning Everard, Randall and the persecution of Familists during the civil wars. Niclaes' publications are now exceedingly rare. The largest collection of English translations appears to be at Cambridge in the University library, but both the British Museum and the Union Theological Seminary possess a considerable number. Representative writings are *An Introduction to the Holy Understanding of the Glasse of Righteousnesse* and *Terra Pacis*, both translated and published in English about 1575, and reprinted in 1649. The latter deserves some note as an allegorical pilgrimage anticipating *Pilgrim's Progress*.

[36] Stephen Denison, *The White Wolfe*, 1627.

nomian doctrine was from time to time attended by religious extravagances of one kind or another, Messianic obsessions, sexual aberrations, outbursts of a kind of symbolic or ritualistic nudism, and other practices which provoked curiosity and condemnation more violent than discerning. Antinomians in general were supposed to be related to a primitive sect of Adamites, and their contemporaries got a certain satisfaction in letting imagination run upon the excesses, particularly sexual, to which they were supposed to be addicted.

That Walwyn came under the influence of Niclaes and his followers seems not improbable. Niclaes's writings are prolix and cloudy with mystical imagery, but not chaotic or irrational. Within the man's often finely poetical rhapsody, there is a core of idealistic social criticism which should have been wholly congenial to one of Walwyn's temper. Niclaes has sympathy for the poor and oppressed. His independent and imaginative mind has kindled to the idealism of Christian faith. He is one of those who seek to redress the balance of this world by rescuing Christianity from the service of the conquerors, and by making its institutions accord with brotherhood and what he called equity. Like other Antinomians, Niclaes would have us believe that the evils we suffer are due to remediable causes, to the ignorance and error in which men are kept by a church imposed by tyrants, tyrants who are their own worst victims. He soon takes flight, of course, from this solid earth. He can see no escape from ignorance and error, save through a mystical experiencing of divine love to be attained by the very modes of religion associated with the divisive social forces he wishes to destroy. He professes to scorn those who cry, "We have it, we are the Congregation of Christ, we are Israel, lo here it is, lo there it is, this is truth, here Christ, there Christ." But he can conceive of a new society only as a renewed church, and therefore in spite of himself only as a secession or sect. Thus he dwindles, lost in dreams of the new Jerusalem, to another seer in a corner.

This was not to be the case with William Walwyn. The

problem as he saw it was to rescue the revolutionary spirit from mysticism and sectarianism by converting both to rational and secular purposes. At a later time, when his plans had been defeated, he would have bitter things to say concerning the "German madde mans Divinity," as well as about those who presumed like Niclaes to be "Goded with God, and Christed with Christ." [37] But in 1642, Walwyn saw in the mystical doctrine of love a possible basis for a new society which should be at the same time civil and catholic. He was familiar with the naturalistic Utopia of Montaigne's cannibals, and with the antique city-state of Plutarch and Thucydides. He admired the Swiss cantons. Might not the yearnings of the sects, which he had taken such pains to observe but not to participate in, prove to be such a force as could be turned, not into still another sect, but into a political movement endeavoring a return to nature and to antique republicanism? *The Power of Love*, together with *Some Considerations* of the previous year, marked the first stage of Walwyn's effort in that direction. The controversial aim was to rouse the people to resist the bishops and the crown. The course taken was to warn men against dissensions caused by attacks of the clergy upon the heresies of the sects. The argument is characteristic. It is first to inquire what are these heresies and who are these sects, in fact the worst heresy of the worst sect, namely the Family of Love. He then gives an acute and eloquent statement of the doctrine of universal love and grace. But he makes this the basis for united action in the public interest, not for winning converts to Familism. Free justification lets men know that they need not curry favor with prelates and clergymen. Love unites them in the common cause against the tyranny of the king. There, for the present, the case rests, but Walwyn would not remain content with the refutation of prelatists and royalists. The ground was prepared to enlist men to fight as brothers against any who should oppose them, even Parliament itself.

[37] *Vanitie.* The German madman here referred to may, of course, be Jakob Boehme.

VI

THE APPEAL TO PUBLIC OPINION

THOMAS GOODWIN, PHILIP NYE, SIDRACH SIMPSON, JEREMIAH BURROUGHS, AND WILLIAM BRIDGE

An Apologeticall Narration [38]

The pamphlet war of 1643 pointed unmistakably to the emergence of public opinion as a decisive factor in public life. To most men in 1644, however, the prime instrument for directing the people in the way they should go was still the church. The contention of all elements of the Puritan party had been that prelacy sought to render the people subservient to the oppressions of the crown. Having suppressed prelacy, Parliament was expected to reform the church in whatever might, if that were possible, come to be regarded as the public interest. This was indeed a thorny problem, not alone because of the difficulty of deciding precisely how God intended the church to be governed, but because of the persistent intrusion of the question whether, or at least to what extent, the church itself should govern. Let the church be ruled howsoever it might, it had still to cope as never before with the rivalry of tub preachers, agitators, demagogues, pamphleteers, scholars and poets — men gifted somehow with the art of discourse and the fortunate opportunities of city crowds and the cheap press.

Parliament had itself already learned that to abolish prelacy was not enough, so long as prelatists could go on publishing arguments against the authority of Parliament. With the sweeping away of the powers which had sought to crush Prynne and his associates in 1637, the Stationers' Company

[38] Vol. II, p. 305.

had been left without support from the government adequate
to maintain its rights of censorship and copyright. Notwithstanding parliamentary resolutions in their behalf, the Stationers were moved in 1643 to file a *Remonstrance* (April)
demanding the appointment of regular licensers with authority
to control rigorously whatever might be printed. "Within
these last four yeers, the affairs of the Presse have grown
very scandalous and enormious." Presses have been set up "in
divers obscure Corners of City and Suburbs" by drapers,
carmen and others. "Sempsters" and other "Emissaries of
such base condition" sell pamphlets on the streets, printed
with "despicable Letters" on "base paper." In many cases
these have been penned elsewhere and then printed, or reprinted, and sold in London. Thus unlicensed printing "by
deceiving the multitude" has in the opinion of the Stationers
"been the fewell in some measure of this miserable Civill-
Warre." Parliament responded to these representations by an
order (June 14) forbidding any publication "unlesse the same
be first approved and licensed under the hands of such person
or persons as both or either of the said Houses shall appoint."
The attribution by Thomason of the Stationers' *Remonstrance*
to Henry Parker is significant. The arm of the law was summoned to aid the pen in the argument against royalist and
prelatist pamphleteers.[39]

[39] Concerning the former laws for the regulation of the press, which under-
went complete break-down after the assembling of the Long Parliament, see
above p. 9, n. 2. During the first three years of the Revolution, great numbers of pamphlets of all sorts went without license or registration in the
books of the Stationers' Company. Not only the clandestine presses, but freemen
of the Company, had disregarded the regulations, and many of the latter are
said to have reprinted books formerly registered by other members of the Stationers' Company. In 1641 and 1642 Parliament made a series of ineffectual
attempts to correct these conditions, sometimes directing the Stationers' Company
to be more vigilant, sometimes condemning particular books or calling particular
authors or publishers to account. Parliament finally adopted the Ordinance for
Printing of June 1643, which provided that no book might be printed unless
first licensed by a special licenser appointed by Parliament, and entered in the
Register of the Stationers' Company. The ordinance reasserted the right of
the Stationers' Company to search for and seize illegal publications. The text
of the printing ordinance of 1643 will be found in the edition of Milton's
Areopagitica in "Arber's English Reprints." See also Masson, *Milton*, III,
265-270.

The anxieties which led to the adoption of the printing ordinance compelled Parliament at about the same time (June 12) also to take steps toward the reorganization of the church. An Assembly of Divines was summoned, not to establish, but to advise Parliament in the establishment of, a reformed church government. The Assembly convened on July 1, dominated from the start by the Puritan clergy, who were determined to make themselves undisputed heirs to the lapsed or endangered powers of the church and to approve nothing short of a system by which all the forces of society were to be brought to bear to compel obedience to church discipline. Needless to say, these men would have nought of the Antinomian notion that men were not naturally depraved and inclined, when left to themselves, unfailingly to sin. Few men alive would have denied that the well-being of all men both here and hereafter depended directly upon the maintenance in some fashion by the church of its authority over faith, worship and morals. Few would have questioned that the neglect of discipline by the church had been the cause, as its reëstablishment would be the remedy, of all the evils which had befallen the country. To the majority of the divines of the Assembly, the situation before them could have but one meaning, namely, that the salvation of England awaited the immediate adoption of the Presbyterian system of uniform centralized control over the teaching and practice of religion.

The uncompromising attitude of the Presbyterians on this point worked a division in the Puritan party fatal in the end to their own cause. It alienated the Independents and drove them into alignment with the sects, thus providing the latter with invaluable countenance and support. It handed over Independents and sectaries alike to be the natural audience or prey, the allies and encouragers, of all daring discontented spirits, rationalistic radicals, visionary mystics and anticlerical agitators of whatever persuasion in religion. All these divers elements it brought together upon the single issue of toleration, providing revolutionary spirits with opportunity to go far in advancing ideas which there could be no hope practically of fulfilling. The crisis was precipitated in January, 1644, by the publication of *An Apologeticall Narration* (January 3), by Thomas Goodwin, Philip Nye, Sidrach Simpson, Jeremiah Burroughs, and William Bridge. The "five dissenting brethren" were educated clergymen in good standing who had gone out from under the Laudian tyranny to serve English congregations, necessarily self-governing and independent of parochial boundaries, in Holland. Returning from exile upon the outbreak of the Revolution with something of the distinction of martyrdom, they had found congregations at home with which they naturally expected to follow a similar course. They represented, no doubt, the same aversion for undue interference in men's private affairs which expressed itself more vigorously in John Goodwin. When they took their places in the Westminster Assembly, therefore, they found themselves the spokesmen for Independent opposition to Presbyterianism. Of the utmost respectability themselves, orthodox in doctrine, moderate in temper, they nevertheless opposed the rigorous centralization of control desired by their opponents, and favored a somewhat larger freedom for individual ministers and congregations. Nothing was further from their thoughts than to aid and encourage sects and freethinkers in general. They even participated, along with fifteen other members of the Assembly, in the publication of *Certaine Considerations to Dis-swade Men from further Gathering of Churches* (December 28), 1643. This was a plea to the people to refrain for the time being from joining or forming independent congregations, and to adhere to the church in the expectation that Parliament would presently establish a rule which all men could with good conscience accept.

Notwithstanding all their cautious moderation, however, the five brethren soon became convinced that they could hope for nothing from the Assembly save to be voted down, and rather than accept the will of the majority of their fellow divines, they forthwith appealed to Parliament and the public.

An Apologeticall Narration, written with studied restraint, made no general plea for religious liberty. Its authors deplored heresy and schism. Nevertheless, its publication was a strategic act of major importance. In a matter affecting the church, the Apologists appealed from the assembled clergy to the civil magistrate, and by publishing their appeal in the press, they carried their case over the heads of Parliament and Assembly alike to the public at large. Nothing could have brought home more sharply to the bewildered defenders of vested interest the dangerous power which had been put into the hands of any who could wield a pen. It seemed an attempt to supersede the Holy Ghost by Demos.

The controversy provoked by *The Apologeticall Narration* reveals the diverse elements of discontent which now coalesced and became vocal in support of toleration. For the intolerance of the Presbyterians, it is easy to be uncritically scornful. Liberty is never an end in itself, and the Westminster divines were not wholly unreasonable in demanding to know what ends it was in this case intended to serve. The Apologists themselves were admittedly well-meaning, but John Goodwin and the bolder Independents, aggressive and none too orthodox rivals of the Presbyterian clergy, promptly came to the Apologists' support with the request that they too be tolerated. Roger Williams and the Anabaptists were ready with anarchic notions of separation of church and state. Walwyn, still anonymously rationalizing the mysticism of the sects, urged toleration as the basis for a democratic state. Henry Robinson argued that persecution was bad for trade. To be sure, all agreed that nothing should be tolerated which was dangerous to the state. But what was dangerous to the state? Moreover, what kind of state? This was a question which would presently grow momentous, for, lurking behind the movement for toleration, were no one knew what wild schemes for political revolution. Under the circumstances, therefore, it was not surprising that the Presbyterians should hold fast to their conviction that the greatest certain danger lay in any move toward the abandonment of public responsibility for the maintenance of religion as the basis of stability in politics and morals.

Space permits here to distinguish only the main currents in the turbid stream of controversy which raged through the year 1644. The Scottish commissioners to the Westminster Assembly promptly countered *The Apologeticall Narration* with *Reformation of Church Government in Scotland Cleered* (January 24). Robert Baillie preached a sermon to the House of Commons, called *Satan the Leader in chief to all who resist the Reparation of Sion* (February 28). Unless Sion be repaired after the Scotch fashion, he is certain that millions will "live as they list, in Blasphemy and Drunkennesse, Chambering and Wantonnesse, Strife and Envy, Ignorance and Impiety," and that heresy will run like a "gangreen," a "canker," from city to city. The exasperation of the majority is, however, first fully expressed by Adam Steuart in *Some Observations and Annotations* (February 29), largely reiterated by Alexander Forbes in *An Anatomy of Independency* (June 14), and by Thomas Edwards in *Antapologia* (July 13). Sermons against toleration were preached by Richard Vines on *The Impostures of Seducing Teachers* (April 23), by Thomas Hill on *The Good old Way, Gods Way* (April 24), and on *The Season for Englands Selfe-Reflection* (August 13), and by Herbert Palmer on *The Glasse of Gods Providence* (August 13). Other diatribes from clerical pens were John Geree's *Vindiciae Ecclesiae Anglicanae* (October 19), Ephraim Pagitt's *The Mysticall Wolfe* (November 24), and Samuel Rutherford's *Due Right of Presbyteries*. Of far greater note, however, was the fact that the exalted Prynne came to the defense of authority with *Twelve Considerable Serious Questions* (September 16) and *Independency Examined* (September 26).

The five apologists, who had provoked all this flow of printer's ink, seem to have refrained as a matter of policy from contributing much to it subsequently, but the bolder

Independents were quick to take the cue. An anonymous writer tried persuasion on the Scotch commissioners in *A Coole Conference* (March 4), to which Steuart published an *Answer* (April 16), which in turn incurred reply in *C. C. The Covenanter Vindicated* (May 2). Steuart himself was meanwhile dealt with at length in the anonymous *M. S. to A. S. with a Plea for Liberty of Conscience in a Church Way* (two editions: May 3, July 11), attributed at the time to John Goodwin but possibly the work of some of his followers.[40] This provoked a tremendous *Duply* from Steuart in two parts, called *Zerubbabel to Sanballat and Tobiah* (Part II, December 4; Part I, March 17, second edition), not to mention frequent passing rejoinders in other pamphlets. Forbes was met by *The Anatomist Anatomis'd* (June 28), 1644, of Sidrach Simpson, Edwards by *A New Yeares Gift* (January 2), 1645, from Katherine Chidley, though his bitterest antagonist, John Goodwin, did not overtake him with *Anapologesiates Antapologias* until (August 27), 1646.

[40] The second edition was called *A Reply of two of the Brethren. . . . Formerly called M. S. to A. S.* Thomason attributed the work to John Goodwin. Masson, *Milton*, III, 121, quotes Baillie's statement, "M. S. against A. S. is John Goodwin." Goodwin says it was written by another pen "ingaged in the same warfare" (*Innocencies Triumph*). Though Pease, *Leveller Movement*, 65 n., inclines to accept the attribution to Goodwin, I prefer to accept Goodwin's own statement. The work expresses the views of Goodwin's circle, but is more loosely argued than was customary with him. He did not generally conceal his authorship, and no reason appears for his having done so in this case. He delivered his mind more characteristically on the whole question in *Theomachia* (October 7).

VII

THE "INDEPENDENT" DOCTRINE OF TOLERATION

JOHN GOODWIN

Θεομαχία [41]

By the publication of Θεομαχία; [42] *Or the Grand Imprudence of Men running the hazard of Fighting against God* (October 7), 1644, John Goodwin first openly entered the fray which had been initiated by *The Apologeticall Narration*. He made what was the boldest and ablest statement which had yet appeared of the principle of toleration seen from the strictly Independent point of view. *Theomachia* immediately confirmed its author's position as the chief exponent of Independency in the press, and as the chief object of attack by the Presbyterians. Prynne at once animadverted upon it in the *Full Reply* (October 19), which he made to *Certain Briefe Observations* (October 4) on his own earlier tracts. These *Observations*, probably emanating from Goodwin's circle, were supported a little later by a *Moderate Answer* (January 27), 1645, to Prynne. [43] Goodwin himself defended *Theomachia* in *Innocencies Triumph* (October 26), 1644. This drew Prynne's fire again in *Truth Triumphing* (January 2), 1645, to which Goodwin fired back in *Innocency and Truth* (January 8), and *Calumny Arraign'd* (January 31). But the matter did not rest there. During the bitter struggle of the immediately ensuing years, *Theomachia* repeatedly appears in the pages of Prynne,

[41] Vol. III, p. 1.

[42] The title was generally referred to as *Theomachia*.

[43] These anonymous tracts have been assigned to Goodwin and to Henry Robinson (*Thomason Catalogue; Dictionary of National Biography*, article on Robinson). Though Robinson did write an *Answer* to Prynne (see below, p. 68), neither of the above pamphlets is in his particular vein. Goodwin himself controverted Prynne at this time in two acknowledged tracts, *Innocencies Triumph* and *Calumny Arraign'd* (see above).

Gillespie, Baillie, Edwards, Vicars and other Presbyterian writers, as one of the chief of Goodwin's offenses and a major document of Independency.

Theomachia is not an argument for absolute freedom of thought and expression. Its professed purpose is to hold up the recent defeat of the Parliamentary army in Cornwall as evidence of God's displeasure with the Assembly. But the strategic exigency of the moment made Goodwin the prime exponent of a theological formula of liberty advantageous to all the radical sects and parties. He thrust forward a text which was to ring through most of the subsequent controversy over toleration. This was found in the words of Gamaliel to the Pharisees on behalf of the Apostles (*Acts* 5:38), "For if this counsell or work be of men, it will come to nought; but if it be of God, yee cannot destroy it, lest yee be found even fighters against God." Goodwin does not go so far as to say that no opinion can ever be proved heretical, but he takes the bold stand that something of God nevertheless inheres in every "Way, Doctrine or Practice" which truly comes from him. To suppress without "proof upon proof, demonstration upon demonstration, evidence upon evidence" anything professed to be derived from God is, therefore, to run the hazard of fighting against God. If it be indeed not from God, God himself in his own time and way, for example by the defeat of an army or by the winnowing of debate, will make plain. And what form of church government, he triumphantly demands, searches out truth and untruth so assiduously as the Independent? He postpones rather than denies ultimate arrival at dogmatic certainty, but this fine point was quickly lost to sight. Goodwin offered what his age regarded as a respectable rational footing to every conventicle of heretics in the land. More than that, though this probably never entered his mind, he was also preparing the way for Walwyn, Lilburne and Overton to claim that there was much of God in the principles of political democracy.

In any case, *Theomachia* brought sharply to view realities

which could not be ignored. Lilburne would soon spring up
again and confirm Goodwin's apt citation of Tacitus' observation that "to punish men of parts and wit is to cast a spirit of
Authority upon them and to make their reputation glowe."
Many an enterprising man of business in the City was ready
to agree with Goodwin that men should not be bound to the
monopoly of the parish church, but freely choose their pastors
and their churches as they did their trades and corporations.
Yet the man was unable wholly to escape the influence of his
cloth. His discourse had to be by firsts and secondlies, creep-
ing like that of any other school divine out to the tip of every
twig of his dialectic. He must still reason from the assumption
that the wisdom, even the expediency, of any act could be
established, if its exact correspondence to scriptural pattern
were but demonstrated. What gave him the advantage over
his clerical opponents was that he was a man of far livelier
imagination than they. The syllogisms of the divine became
often but a form of imaginative intuition. Goodwin could
develop with damaging vividness the apt analogy between
Pharisee and Presbyterian, Apostle and Independent preacher.
He was more sensitive than most theological debaters to the
public mind, and adhered more closely to the purpose of
persuasion. It was no wonder that Edwards in his second
Gangraena should have turned upon the author of *Theomachia* as the "great Rabbi and Seraphicall Doctor," the "hairy
rough wilde red man," the "Goliah," the "great red dragon"
of revolution.

VIII

TOLERATION AND THE SECTS

[WILLIAM WALWYN]
The Compassionate Samaritane [44]

ROGER WILLIAMS
The Bloudy Tenent of Persecution [45]

The alliance between the Independents and the sectaries and radicals in support of liberty of conscience was only temporary. It was destined to dissolve so soon as the menace of persecution was removed from the congregations and their pastors. The followers of John Goodwin could envisage independent churches but not a free society. They could not reach the conception of the state as an institution devoted purely to the welfare of citizens without reference to their godliness. They were moving from the start, not toward the democracy of the Levellers, but toward the rule of the saints of the Barebones Parliament, such a rule as had already attempted to establish itself in New England and had there engendered its first rebel.

Yet for the time being in England, saints and democrats found common interest in setting up their claim to be tolerated beside the five Apologists. Speaking once more for the Separatists, William Walwyn was ready to confirm the worst fears of the Presbyterians that the *Apologeticall Narration* would raise the hopes of all enemies of discipline. Roger Williams was at hand to do the same. Williams had just returned in quest of legal recognition for what amounted to an Antinomian Utopia in the wilderness, erected in the very face of

[44] Vol. III, p. 59.
[45] Williams's principal works have been republished in the *Narragansett Club Publications*, I-VI, 1866-1874. *The Bloudy Tenent* also appears in *Tracts on Liberty of Conscience*, published by the Hanserd Knollys Society.

Or

A DISCOVERY OF THE MOST
DANGEROVS AND DAMNABLE TENETS
THAT HAVE BEEN SPREAD WITHIN THIS FEW
yeares: By many Erronious, Heriticall and Mechannick fpirits. By which the very foundation of Chriftian knowledge
and practife is endeavoured to be overturned.

THAT Chrifts righteoufnefle was a beggarly righteoufnefle.

2. That Chrifts blood did not purchafe Heaven for any man.

3. That Chrift fhed his blood for Kine and Horfes, as well as formen.

4. That the foules of men and divels are mortall, and that none are immortall but God.

5. That we are onely to beleeve the Scriptures, fo far as they are agreeable to fenfe and reafon.

6. That the Scriptures are uncertain and unfufficient, and not an infallible Rule of Faith.

7. That the Scriptures cannot be faid to be the Word of God, becaufe there is no word of God but Chrift.

8. That the Scriptures of the old Teftament do not binde or concern Chriftians under the new.

9. That adultery and drunkennefle is no fin.

10. That Prayer in Families is unlawfull.

11. A company of Souldiers in derifion of Baptifme, baptifed a horfe, having pift in the Font, fprinkled it on the Horfe, and croft him on the Fore-head, and named him Ball-Efau, becaufe he was hairie.

12. That Chrifts fufferings were onely for our examples, and not to purchafe Heaven for m.

13. That Beleevers have nothing to doe to take care, or keep from fin.

14. That no man was caft into hell for fin, but onely becaufe God would have it fo.

15. That Chrift will deftroy all Governments, lawfull and unlawfull.

16. That God was never difpleafed with men for fin; if he were, there were a changeablenefse in God.

17. That the foul of man dies with the body

18. That the Church of England and Miniftery thereof is Anti-chriftian, and of the Devil.

19. That it is the will of God that tolleration of the moft Pagan hereffe, Jewifh, Turkifh, or Antichriftian worfhip be granted to all men in all Nations.

20. That a man may lawfully put away his wife, if fhe might lawfully lye with another man, for fleep was death.

21. That God is the Author of the finfulnefle of his people.

22. That man had life before God breathed it into him.

23. That there is no refurrection of the bodies of men after this life.

24. That if a womans husband was afleep or abfent, fhe might lawfully lye with another man, for fleep was death.

25. That John Baptifts doctrine was a leatherne doctrine.

26. That Adams fin did not deferve hell.

27. That all the children of Adam that die in their infancie fhall be faved.

28. That all the heaven there is, is here on earth.

29. That Johns Baptifme which was of Water, did end at the coming of Chrift.

30. That it is unlawful to fing Pfalmes.

31. That it is blafphemy to fay that there is now any office of the miniftery.

32. That Univerfities is of the Devil, and humane learning is of the flesh.

33. That many fhall be faved that were not elected.

34. That they are the great Antichrift that deny the generall redemption of the whole Creation.

35. That we have no example in all the Gofpel, for Saints to pray with unbeleevers.

36. A Sectary faid, what had any man to do if he worfhipt the Sun or moon, no man had to do with his Confcience.

37. That it is injuftice in God to punifh the foules of the wicked in Hell, whileft their bodies are at reft in their graves, fince both lived together.

38. That all the Heathen fhall be faved, becaufe they are not guilty of unbeleef.

39. That millions of thoufands are damned for a time, and not totally, for not beleeving the Covenant of generall redemption.

40. That the true faith of beleeving the Covenant of generall redemption, though it were but in three perfons, is fufficient to fave all the reft of the Creation.

41. That the Doctrine of repentance is a foule depraving doctrine.

42. That there ought to be no Fafting daies under the Gofpel.

43. That Sanctification is but a Dung-hill, and dirty qualification.

44. That there is no Originall fin in us.

45. That under the daies of the new Teftament all daies are alike to Chriftians, and that the Lords day, or fabbath ought not to be kept.

46. That there is no Church, nor Ordinance nor Miniftery in the world.

47. That it is unlawful to teach children to pray.

48. That Infants fhall never rife againe, becaufe they were not capable of knowing God, and fo not of enjoying God.

49. That there is power in men to refift grace.

Aprill 26.

Printed and Publifhed according to Order. 1647.

THESE TRADESMEN ARE PREACHERS

Reproduced from an original broadside in the Thomason Collection in the British Museum [669 f 11 (6)].

the Utopia of saints at Massachusetts Bay. Born about 1604, the son of a merchant tailor in London, he had been led by the doctrine of free justification to conclusions resembling those of Walwyn, but to a very different fate. Sir Edward Coke had, it would seem, provided for his education. He had gone from Cambridge to serve as chaplain to Sir Edward Masham in Essex. He departed for New England in 1630 with ideas and scruples which prevented advancement at home. Whence these came, it is difficult precisely to say. The influence of Coke may have counted for something. Cambridge was not devoid of liberalism. Lady Masham was the kinswoman of Cromwell, Hampden and Whalley. Before leaving England, Williams had the acquaintance of John Cotton and Thomas Hooker, men who, though destined to oppose him later, had a certain liberality of outlook. In any event, he arrived in Boston early in 1631 with — or so it seemed to the orthodox — a windmill in his head.[46]

The war which Williams waged in New England against the aspirations of Calvinist divines to rule as the elect of God prepared him to take his place in England beside the author of *The Power of Love*. The situations in the two countries, however different in circumstances and the stages of their development, were in certain respects parallel. In Massachusetts, authority was vested from the start in the group of ministers, magistrates and zealous church members, who came determined to found a state upon the law of Moses. The course taken to this end was to push forward the development of a form of church government and religious discipline which, though nominally Independent, was thoroughly Presbyterian in spirit and effect. The people who came to Massachusetts, however, were by no means all saints, and the rigors of that rough country did not breed yielding tempers. The depths of its wilderness offered escape for the hardy and no favors for the elect. As pastor of Salem, Williams soon found him-

[46] James Ernst, *The Political Thought of Roger Williams*, 1929; *Roger Williams*, 1932.

self leader of the opposition to uniformity. The theological expression of that opposition was that the grace of God was dealt equally to all, and not reserved for the few. The practical corollary was that the state owed countenance and support to no body of the elect, to no church, to no doctrine, in fact to no religion, but must secure the liberty of each man in token of the mystical brotherhood of all. Such ideas, expressed as no uncertain demand for toleration and democratic government, could not but be regarded by the rulers of the colony as a challenge to their authority. The "Simple Cobler of Aggawam in America" gave utterance a little later (1647) to the common view that the "New-English" did not wish to be regarded as a "Colluvies of wild Opinionists, swarmed into a remote wilderness to find elbow-roome for phanatick Doctrines and practises." To "all Familists, Antinomians, Anabaptists, and other Enthusiasts," he allowed free liberty to keep away or begone as fast as they could. The General Court ordered Williams to leave the colony, and in January, 1636, he fled to the shores of Narragansett Bay. There, with the gathering about him of a miscellaneous assortment of companions, he initiated what has been hailed as the first attempt to put the principles of freedom into practice. But the repercussions of frontier democracy upon law and order in Massachusetts were such that Williams was forced to betake himself to London to secure legal recognition of the independence of Rhode Island. The younger Vane was his friend and sat with Pym, Cromwell and other notables on the Parliamentary commission which granted (March 14, 1644) a patent for his settlement, authorizing him to set up such government as its inhabitants might choose.

Upon his arrival in London in the summer of 1643, Williams applied himself also to the publication of his *Key into the Language of America* (September 7). He was probably responsible, as well, for the publication in the same year of *A Letter of Mr. Cotton Teacher of the Church in Boston, in New England to Mr. Williams a Preacher there*. This was a defense, addressed to him some time before, of the action of Massachusetts in banishing him. He proceeded to lay his own side of the case before the public in *Mr. Cottons Letter Lately Printed, Examined and Answered* (February 5), 1644. Meanwhile he was regarding with an experienced eye the strivings of the Westminster Assembly over the very issues in which he had been so actively concerned in America. When the dissenting brethren put forth their *Apologeticall Narration*, he was ready to embarrass both parties with *Queries of Highest Consideration* (February 9). These rhetorical questions went directly to the root of the matter. The members of the Assembly, in spite of their alleged infallibility, could come to no agreement, and without the aid of the state, no party of them could impose its will. The state then must perforce choose among religions. But if the rulers of the state were competent to make such a choice, why not the people? Why not every man for himself?

Williams's personal controversy, however, was not with the Assembly, but with Massachusetts, and when he departed again for Rhode Island in September, he left behind him a long reply to John Cotton, called *The Bloudy Tenent of Persecution for cause of Conscience, discussed, in a Conference betweene Truth and Peace* (July 15). This was addressed to Parliament, intended in part, no doubt, to offset future attempts to range the home government against the Rhode Island venture. Cotton in the following year published *The Way of the Churches of Christ in New England* (April 4), and in 1648 *The Way of Congregational Churches cleared* (February 9), cleared, that is, of the suspicion of tolerance. He replied to Williams in *The Bloudy Tenent washed and made white in the bloud of the Lambe* (May 15), 1647, and Williams carried on the controversy in *The Bloudy Tenent yet More Bloudy* (April 28), 1652.

The Bloudy Tenent was one of the most widely condemned works of the time. Baillie, Gillespie, Pagitt, Prynne and Edwards, all called anathema upon it. It owes little of its

fame in later times to literary merit. Williams had at all costs
to refute John Cotton. He does so in the conventional manner,
unable to escape polemic, to think of his reader rather than
of his antagonist. Only now and then in the long-winded
dialogue between Truth and Peace does discourse move
straight and clear. Nevertheless, the application of the doctrine of free justification and spiritual equality to the reconstruction of society does transpire. Prefaced to the whole is a
remarkable statement of the principle of toleration from
which, Williams thought, reconstruction must proceed. It
summed up in unequivocal terms the practical logic of the
mystical ideas of the sects concerning church and state. It was
particularly responsible for the reiteration of opprobrium
which fell upon the whole work. The single assertion that
God intended Jews, Pagans, Turks, and unchristian consciences in general to be opposed by no sword save that of
the spirit was enough of itself to invite damnation from minds
which were incapable of comprehending Williams's argument
in its entirety.

The Bloudy Tenent was perhaps the most extreme statement of the theory of natural rights which had yet appeared.
That it was the source, as some have thought, from which
flowed all later expressions of that theory, can hardly receive
sober credence.[47] In the circles in which Williams moved before
his emigration in 1630, in the circles in which Walwyn moved
prior to 1640 and in which the two men may easily have
crossed paths, the doctrine of free justification was common
matter for serious discussion. The moment a clash arose between centralized authority and the dynamic forces of individ-

[47] Masson, *Milton*, III, 112-120, attaches great importance to *The Bloudy
Tenent*, but Masson is much given to hero worship, and had not actually read
very widely in the pamphlet literature of the time. Ernst (see above), in his
Political Thought of Roger Williams, 26, reviews the assertions of later writers
concerning the influence of Williams, but is himself wisely non-committal. This
is not the case in his later *Roger Williams and the English Revolution* (Rhode
Island Historical Society Collections, XXIV, 1931) and his *Roger Williams*,
1932. He there interprets contemporary assertions of the doctrine of liberty as
specific evidence of the direct influence of *The Bloudy Tenent*, even of direct
allusion to Williams himself.

ualism, the doctrine of free justification was certain to undergo restatement and to emerge as the theory of toleration and natural rights. This was what happened when Salem under Williams's leadership undertook to resist the General Court of Massachusetts. This was also what happened when spokesmen for the sects in England saw in the dispute over Independency occasion to oppose the coercive power of the church. Those men may very likely have had prompt and frequent contact with Williams upon his return, but the evidence of that fact is of the vaguest. They had already gone far in their ideas without him, and could hardly have stood in need of light from Rhode Island. Williams did not launch the movement, though he did put in a timely and effective oar.

At the very moment when *The Bloudy Tenent* was appearing from the press, Walwyn, it would seem, was presenting his own plea for freedom and toleration. This was an anonymous tract called *The Compassionate Samaritane*, printed without license some time in 1644.[48] The tiny pamphlet, dedicated to the House of Commons, was divided into two parts. The first part after the dedication (pages 7-71) was headed *Liberty of Conscience Asserted and the Separatist Vindicated*, the second (pages 72-83) *Good Counsell to all*. The work is a statement of Walwyn's characteristic objections to the attitude which had been taken by the Apologists toward the sects and "gathered churches " not only in the *Apologeticall Narration* but even more particularly in the *Certaine Considerations* which they had put forth in conjunction with some of their Presbyterian colleagues.[49] Walwyn probably published *The Compassionate Samaritane* shortly after the appearance of Thomas Bakewell's *Confutation of Anabaptists* (June 21), and seems to have issued a second edition almost immediately.

He turns upon the questions raised by the Apologists the point of view which he had already expressed in *Some Considerations* and *The Power of Love*. His immediate purpose

[48] For evidence of the date of publication and of Walwyn's authorship, see Appendix A.
[49] See above, p. 49.

was to remonstrate against the exclusion of the Separatists from toleration by Apologists and Presbyterians alike. He again takes pains to state that he himself is not a sectary. Religious freedom was for him the way to a larger freedom than simple tolerance, and it is this which gives to his pamphlet its peculiar interest. For Walwyn, the rejection of belief in human depravity and the acceptance of natural goodness meant the assumption that nature had planted reason in the breasts of common men. To be sure, reason was fallible, and, whether reasonable or not, men often differed. But with good will and charity, by patient search behind appearances and professions, by rational discussion and appeal, they could be brought to a common reason, to a common understanding, that is, of common needs such as were attainable by common effort. The true end was not the toleration of the sect or congregation, but the free flourishing of the commonwealth. Government, stripped of adventitious circumstances and rendered accessible without fear or favor to the appeal of reason and of reason alone, was properly nothing but the means to that end. The impediment was always the special interest of the few opposed to that of the commonwealth. That interest appeared for the moment in the selfish aggression of the clergy. The clergy clouded the understanding of the people in order to set them at variance with one another. The clergy sought to make common men believe themselves too ignorant and depraved to understand the Bible unaided. They pretended, though disagreeing among themselves on the points of faith, to be alone competent to tell other men what to believe. They sought to engross all preaching, and now too all printing, to themselves, as though the ministry were not a trade like any other, such as that of the merchant, the bookseller or the tailor. And what did they in their infallibility profess to teach? Mainly that men who follow reason are to be feared, hated and persecuted as heretics. What the clergy really wanted was the power lately wrested from the prelates and the aggrandizement of private interests precisely similar to those which common men, Separatists not least, were at the very moment shedding their blood to overthrow. In these circumstances, Walwyn thought it his own duty to protest on the Separatists' behalf to the House of Commons, "without boldnesse and without feare," "well assured, that as it is mine, and every mans duty, to furnish You with what we conceive will advance the Common good, or bring ease or comfort to any sort of men that deserve well of their Countrey . . . , so likewise it is Your duty to heare and put in execution, whatsoever to Your judgments shall appeare conducing to those good ends and purposes."

IX

THE UTOPIA OF FREE SPEECH AND FREE TRADE

[HENRY ROBINSON]
Liberty of Conscience [50]

JOHN MILTON
Areopagitica [51]

While democracy and nonconformity in the persons of Walwyn, Williams and Goodwin were raising voices against intolerance, a no less ominous protest was also being registered on behalf of emergent capitalist enterprise. This was the work of Henry Robinson. Though sympathetic with the demands of the Independents, he seems to have kept clear of all religious groups and movements. Neither did he participate in political agitation. His affiliation was rather with Samuel Hartlib, whose physiocratic ideas and schemes enlisted Robinson's active interest and support. Walwyn a little later speaks rather scornfully of "nimble-pated Mr. Robinson," one of "our inventing innovating travellers." [52] Hartlib's *Description of the famous Kingdome of Macaria* (October 25), 1641, depicted an ideal state, concerned chiefly with the advancement of economic production. On the subject of toleration, which was taken for granted in Macaria, Robinson came to Hartlib's support in 1644 in a friendly exchange of letters with John Dury. [53] But his real objective revealed itself in

[50] Vol. III, p. 105.

[51] *The Works of John Milton*, Columbia University Press, 1931, Volume IV.

[52] *Juries Justified*. See *Dictionary of National Biography*, article on Robinson by W. A. Shaw, with information supplied by C. H. Firth; also Firth, *English Historical Review*, IX, 715-717; and Shaw, *Select Tracts and Documents Illustrative of English Monetary History*.

[53] John Dury (1596-1680), a kind of seventeenth-century internationalist, had been educated abroad, served as minister to various English congregations on the continent and as tutor to Princess Mary of Orange. In *A Summary Discourse concerning the work of Peace Ecclesiastical*, 1641, and in subsequent

1650, when he endeavored to put into practice the proposal for a kind of information bureau and labor exchange, or "office of addresses and encounters," which Hartlib had made in his *Considerations tending to the Happy Accomplishment of Englands Reformation in Church and State* (May), 1647.

No less than other men of his time, Robinson was a single-minded enthusiast, but the promised land toward which he desired to lead his countrymen was a capitalist empire. Government, law, religion and social institutions should foster individual enterprise for labor, production and trade, so that "all manner of people may get a livelyhood with cheerfulness and a good Conscience." "I conceive it will appeare upon inquiry," he writes upon the first page of his *Brief Considerations Concerning the Advancement of Trade and Navigation*:

1. That in whatsoever Country the greatest stock of money and

---

works, he dedicated himself to the effort to unite the Protestant churches of Europe, a project to which Hartlib also lent his aid in *A Briefe Relation of that which hath been lately attempted to procure Ecclesiasticall Peace*, 1641, published in "Harleian Miscellany," and in other tracts. Like Hartlib, Dury also interested himself in education, publishing *The Reformed School* in 1650. In 1644, he addressed *An Epistolary Discourse* (August 15) to Thomas Goodwin, Phillip Nye and Hartlib, endeavoring to make peace between the Presbyterians and their opponents. *An Answer to Mr. John Dury* (August 17) has been attributed to Robinson (*Dictionary of National Biography*), but probably emanated from someone more closely identified with the Independents. Robinson's answer (dated November 5, 1644) appears in *Some Few Considerations* (July 18), 1646, which also contains letters addressed by Dury to Robinson and to "Mr. H," probably Hartlib. Robinson refers to Hartlib as his worthy friend, and was also on friendly terms with Dury. Hartlib's friendship with Milton is well known. Dury also seems to have had some acquaintance with the poet, a copy of whose *Eikonoklastes* is preserved in the British Museum with "*Ex dono Authoris, John Dury*" on the title-page, though not in Milton's hand. I have found no evidence that Milton also knew Robinson, or that he took any active interest in the economic projects which the latter shared with Hartlib. That the desire of Dury, Hartlib and Robinson to find some neutral ground upon which religious differences might be composed was shared by others is evidenced in *A Short Letter* (September 14) addressed by Hartlib to Hezekiah Woodward, requesting the latter's opinion of Edwards's *Antapologia*. This was published with Woodward's "large and modest Answer," a confused plea for tolerance chiefly interesting for its unacknowledged allusion to Sir Thomas Browne's *Religio Medici*: "I could never, saith one, divide myselfe from any upon the difference of an opinion; or be angry with his judgement for not agreeing with mine in that, from which, perhaps, within a few dayes, I should dissent myselfe." See *Religio Medici*, 1642, 11.

credit shall be raised; there will the greatest Trade of the world be established.

2. That the greatest Trade of one Country, hath a Capacity of undermining, and eating out the lesser Trades of any other Countryes.

3. That the greatest Trade will be able to make the greatest number of shipping. And,

4. That what Nation soever can attaine to and continue the greatest Trade, and number of shipping, will get and keepe the Soveraignty of the Seas, and consequently the greatest Dominion of the World.

Born about 1605, the son of a mercer and himself admitted to the Mercers' Company in 1626, Robinson spent part at least of his young manhood in Constantinople, Italy, the Low Countries and elsewhere on the Continent. Returning to England sometime before the outbreak of the civil wars, he undertook to transpose the principles of Macaria into terms of public policy for England. His first pamphlet bears the significant title, *Englands Safetie in Trades Encrease* (August), 1641.[54] It ignores the religious and political convulsions of the moment in order to urge upon Parliament measures for the expansion of manufacture, fishing, trade, shipping, plantation in America, and for the establishment of a system of financial credit and exchange. It also proposes that the vexed question of the ethics of usury be settled by the advice of merchants as well as of churchmen. In *Libertas, or Reliefe to the English Captives in Algier* (October), 1641, Robinson followed up these proposals by another for sending the fleet to clear the Mediterranean for English shipping and to block up the Grand Turk in Constantinople. Here was no provincial zealot or insular reformer but an imperial Englishman.

As soon as some end to civil strife appeared to sight in 1650, Robinson was ready to resume his argument that the country get on with the business of its destiny. He then published *Briefe Considerations Concerning the Advancement of Trade and Navigation, Humbly tendred unto all ingenious Patriots; Purposely to incite them to endeavour the felicitie of*

[54] Reprinted by Shaw, see above, p. 64, n. 52.

this Nation, by contributing their Assistance towards the Enlargement of Trade, and Navigation as the most sure foundation (January 8), 1650. He announced (September 7), 1650, his *Office of Addresses and Encounters* in Threadneedle Street, as a place

where all people of each Rancke and Quality may receive directions and advice for the most cheap and speedy way of attaining whatsoever they can lawfully desire. Or, the only Course for poor people to get speedy employment, and to keep others from approaching poverty, for want of Employment. To the multiplying of Trade, the advancement of Navigation, and establishing the famous City of London in a more plentiful and flourishing Condition than ever.

Under the Commonwealth, Robinson continued to press for the encouragement of individual enterprise, urging especially reforms for the simplification of the law and of the administration of justice.[55] He served the Commonwealth as Auditor of the Excise. After the Restoration, we hear of him applying for a patent on a device for extinguishing fires and preserving ships.

The attitude of such a man toward the questions raised by the *Apologeticall Narration* may be read in his anonymous pamphlet, *Liberty of Conscience* (March 24), 1644.[56] The controversies raging about him seem to have convinced Robinson that Englishmen could not be persuaded to attend to their real interests so long as they permitted themselves to be distracted by partisan appeals to their religious convictions.

[55] *Certain Considerations in order to a more speedy, cheap, and equall distribution of Justice* (November 14), 1651, answered by Walwyn in *Juries Justified* (December 2); *Certain Proposals in order to the Peoples Freedome*, 1652 (selections reprinted by Shaw, see above, p. 64, n. 52); *Certain Proposals in order to a new modelling of the Lawes and Law Proceedings*, 1653.

[56] Edwards, *Gangraena*, I, 96, says that Robinson "is commonly reported to be the Author of that Book called *Liberty of Conscience.*" This attribution was first cited and confirmed by Firth (see above, p. 64, n. 52). For the suggestion that Walwyn may have had a hand in the work, see Appendix A. I have no hesitation in assigning *Liberty of Conscience, John the Baptist, An Answer to Mr. William Prynnes Twelve Questions, A Short Answer to A. S.,* and *The Falsehood of Mr. William Pryns Truth Triumphing,* to Robinson. These tracts give similar evidence that their author had lived abroad as a merchant, and the point of view, affected in each case by that fact, can be attributed to no one but Robinson.

If we can believe Prynne,[57] his response to the situation was to set up a press of his own for the printing of unlicensed books, printers being brought from Amsterdam for the purpose. He did in any case get *Liberty of Conscience* published, and followed that by other tracts reiterating the argument so peculiarly his own. *John the Baptist* (September 23) buttressed his reasoning point by point with Scripture.[58] In *An Answer to Mr. William Prynns Twelve Questions* (November 1), *A Short Answer to A. S.* (February 3), 1645, and *The Falsehood of Mr. William Pryns Truth Triumphing* (May 8), 1645, he gave vigorous expression to his exasperation with the parochial bigotry of the Presbyterians, represented by two of their doughtiest champions.

No writer of the time illustrates better than Robinson the manner in which theology in the great revolution was being hoist with its own petard. At the opening of the civil wars, it seemed still solidly entrenched in men's minds as the master science. Every move, every interest, in state and society as well as in the church must still be made to seem rational and just in the terms, scriptural and metaphysical, of some theological system. The effect was to expose the practical inadequacy of theology. Every theological polemic claimed the absolute truth and the universal applicability of its author's system. The interests, however, which sought rational support and expression in theology were the irreconcilable forces of economic, social and national conflict, and no interest but could

[57] *Fresh Discovery*, 9. Prynne also suspected Robinson of being the author of the Martin tracts written by Overton. See below, p. 97.

[58] *John the Baptist* was attacked by Gillespie, *A Late Dialogue* (October 30) and *Wholesome Severity* (January 8), 1645. It is referred to by Robinson himself in *Answer to . . . Prynns Twelve Questions* and *Short Answer to A. S.* Prynne *Fresh Discovery* 4 says that Robinson is the "supposed Author" of *Answer*. Thomason is mistaken in attributing that work to Henry Burton, who shortly after brought out his *Vindication* (November 14). Prynne's incorrect attribution (*loc. cit.*) of *Short Answer* to John Goodwin was no doubt due to the association of the latter with earlier attacks on Steuart (see above, p. 52). *The Falsehood*, attacked by Bastwick in *Independency not Gods Ordinance* and by Edwards in *Gangraena* I, is correctly attributed to Robinson by Prynne (*loc. cit.*). *Certaine Briefe Observations and Antiquaeryes: On Master Prin his Twelve Questions* (see above, p. 53) has been confused in the Thomason Catalogue and elsewhere with *Answer to . . . Prynns Twelve Questions*.

find theologians to square it with the will of God. The inevitable result was to discredit all theologies and creeds in the minds of intelligent people. Robinson is fond of asking what a Turk would do, if he wished to turn Christian. How must he be directed which form of Christianity to yield to? Must it be to all, or to that which has the sharpest sword?[59] Thus theology was itself disrupted by the clash of interests which it professed to comprehend, but served only to foster.

Practical men like Robinson could not but grow sceptical of the pretensions of all creeds; and yet, so much was theology the mental atmosphere of the age, that skepticism itself must needs be initiated in theological terms. Thus Robinson lays hold of the dogma of free conscience as the starting point of an endeavor to immunize men against the claims of creeds for practical support. He is at one with Goodwin, Walwyn, Milton and the rest in asserting the divine right of private judgment. He regards that right, however, as merely another form of the right of private enterprise or of private property. God, we read in *Liberty of Conscience*, has left Scripture liable to many interpretations expressly in order that each man may have opportunity to secure an interpretation of his own. No man can have a natural monopoly of truth, and the more freely each man exercises his own gifts in its pursuit, the more of truth will be discovered and possessed. As "in civill affaires. . . . , every man most commonly understands his owne businesse," as "every man is desirous to doe with his owne as he thinkes good himselfe," and as it would be absurd for the state to make laws requiring men to manage their worldly affairs after one "generall prescript forme and manner," so in religion every man should be permitted to go his own way. Compulsion compels men only to hypocrisy or rebellion. This is Robinson's doctrinal argument, to which, though he constantly returns, he is never able for long at a time to cleave. Scripture is brandished abundantly in *Liberty of Conscience*, still more so in *John the Baptist*, but he is always

[59] *John the Baptist*, 85; *Answer to . . . Prynns Twelve Questions*, 3.

being lured off the theological track by his own lively experience of men and affairs, by some pat analogy in trade, or by
some shrewd observation of human nature in Italy, in Amsterdam, or among the Turks.

Robinson's seesawing in this fashion between two worlds
often works confusion to his writing, but in his thinking it
also produces interesting results. The dogma of free conscience assumed that men do naturally think and choose for
themselves when free from compulsion. But Robinson was
aware of compulsions not merely physical, and of motives
not wholly rational. Granting there can be but one true religion, "who can tell me the precise and just precincts thereof?"
Every man is for the most part of that religion to which he
has been bred.[60] Interest, which we should at the present day
call economic, and not religious zeal is often if not always
the prime motive. Why otherwise should Christendom, "a
spot of ground only," be a cockpit of war, "and all the world
besides but as a breathing space?" The pretended cause of war
and persecution is religion. But nothing is more obvious than
that men cannot and do not hope by such means to make
truth prevail. When Catholics are compelled to go to church in
England, they stop their ears; Protestants, driven to mass
in Italy, send "their eyes gadding after beauty." "A Protestant sermon is as Idolatrous to a Papist, as a Popish Mass is
to a Protestant; and neither of them can more judge with the
understanding, than see with the eyes of the other." [61] "Men
doe not imbrace errours otherwise than as they account
them truths, and therefore 'tis no marvell if they prove as
pertinacious in defence of the one, as they are constant
in defending the other." [62] Nor does God save men by nations;
he says to no Christian people, "I will give unto thee and thy
seed thy neighbours country." The fact is that the real motive
of war and persecution is not religion but covetousness. "War

[60] *Short Answer*, 25-27; *John the Baptist*, 85.
[61] *Short Answer*, 36.
[62] *Answer to . . . Prynns Twelve Questions*, 17.

was never yet without a coveting." "Few have been yet so mad as to put people to death meerly for Religions sake." He who drags the heretic to court, does so for his own "respective benefit and ends." Religion is merely the cloak assumed by covetousness to make itself seem lawful and to compel support. The clergy are, of course, cited as the chief offenders in this respect, since, Robinson alleges, they claim a monopoly to which they are not entitled. It is "as if a Taylor or Hatter should wrench your money from you though you lik'd not, would not have his wares, his services." [63] "He that putteth not into their mouthes, they even prepare War against him."

So far, Robinson's plea is not essentially dissimilar to that of Walwyn, but it takes a strikingly different turn. There were depths of practical illogic in intolerance which only eyes experienced like his could penetrate. If the Westminster Assembly is inspired by the Holy Ghost to dictate true religion to Englishmen, why not to all the world? If to tolerate any but the true religion as revealed by the Holy Ghost to the Westminster Assembly be to partake the sin and hence the danger of other men, then must Englishmen "damn for the most part hand over head" all other Christian professions, nations and peoples, to say nothing of Jews, Mohammedans, Pagans and Christians of the East. "Would it not be wonder if this circumference, this little continent of earth, should satisfie the vaste desires of such, who seem to think, that the Heavens so infinitely more capacious, were only made for them and some few of their familiars?" [64] But if we may not tolerate men of other faiths, how can we ever venture to go among them? How can we permit French Papists, Dutch Anabaptists, Lutherans or Turks, travelers, traders or ambassadors, to come to England? Or if we permit Englishmen to live abroad among such people, or such people to live here, how can we deny to Englishmen in England the liberty they may have abroad, or that we grant to aliens on English soil?

[63] *Short Answer*, 30.   [64] *Short Answer*, 25-27.

Robinson's answer to these questions has two revealing sides. Not for nothing had the author of *Englands Safetie in Trades Encrease* entered upon this dispute. He knew that men are generally of that faith to which they are bred, that each nation thinks its own faith the true one, and he declared that he did not know which was in the right. Nevertheless, he believed that it is the duty of Englishmen to convert the unbelievers and misbelievers of other lands. The first chapter of *John the Baptist* opens with five pages of missionary texts from the New Testament. Conversion was obviously impossible without intercourse, intercourse without tolerance, and throughout the whole argument runs the implication that such also were the conditions necessary for trade and for all that followed in Robinson's teeming mind. The imperialist was stealing the fanatic's thunder. Religion might better be made to serve and sanctify capitalist enterprise than the covetousness of churchmen, and foreign missions be made to give grace to foreign trade.

But to overemphasize what some may see as toleration's feet of clay would be misleading and unjust. England was destined to become not another Geneva nor even a larger Scotland but a new Rome. Robinson read that destiny into the ears of the bigots of his time. It was a still greater distinction on his part to have seen like Milton the liberation of the mind as the noblest part of that destiny.

It is impossible that in a rationall way there should be a firme secure peace throughout the world, nay not in a Province, City or Towne, so long as men make a point of conscience to compell one another to their opinions. . . . It is impossible for a man to hold fast the truth, or be fully perswaded in his owne heart of what he does, of what Religion he makes choice of; unlesse after he hath searched the Scriptures, and try'de the spirits whether they be of God or no, it be lawful for him to reject that which shall appear to him as evill, and adhere to that which seems good in his own judgement and apprehension [*Falsehood*].

Robinson's tracts, like those of his friend Hartlib, were for the time essentially Utopian. The Presbyterians and the Apologists, John Goodwin and his fellow Independents, Walwyn representing the sects, each spoke in behalf of more or less organized efforts for securing political power. Robinson, though lending his weight to the Independents, did not concern himself with politics. He displayed what England might become if her rulers and her clergy would let her, but his prescient notions were not such as could be made serviceable by any party in the actual struggle of the moment. This was no less true of Hartlib's other friend, John Milton. More concerned with spiritual than with business enterprise, the latter had, since his participation in the attack on prelacy, been engaged in teaching and in preparation for a great national poem. Hartlib, indeed, full of the ideas of Comenius, had elicited from him a statement of his notions for educational reform in *Of Education* (June 5), 1644. An interest of long standing in the subject of marriage, followed in 1642 by personal ill fortune in the choice of a wife, had also prompted him to the advocacy of divorce. According to his own statement in the *Second Defence*, this was but a step in a considered campaign for liberty in all fields of life. The abuses committed by the church in the administration of the laws concerning marriage had long been a cause of complaint in the Puritan classes. Milton proposed in *The Doctrine and Discipline of Divorce* (August 1), 1643,[65] that the jurisdiction of the church in this matter be swept away, and that marriage be made a civil contract with freedom of divorce on grounds of incompatibility. When the divines of the Assembly, turning a deaf ear to these proposals, embarked upon their struggle with the Apologists for retention of all ecclesiastical power in their own hands, Milton prepared a second edition of his tract

[65] Followed by *The Judgement of Martin Bucer* (August 6), 1644, and attacked by *An Answer to a book intituled The Doctrine and Discipline of Divorce* (November 19), to which Milton made reply in *Colasterion* (March 4), 1645, further defending his position in *Tetrachordon*, of the same date. B. A. Wright, "Milton's First Marriage," *Modern Language Review*, XXVI, XXVII, has shown that Milton's marriage to Mary Powell must have occurred, not as has been commonly supposed in 1643, but in 1642. See also C. L. Powell's *English Domestic Relations*.

(February 2), 1644. He now added a preface directly addressed to Parliament and the Assembly. It contained the statement that the first duty of rulers was to "know perfectly how far the territory and dominion extends of just and honest liberty." The laws of God should be "considered not altogether by the narrow intellectuals of quotationists and commonplacers," but by men

able to shew us the waies of the Lord strait and faithful as they are, not full of cranks and contradictions, and pitfalling dispenses, but with divine insight and benignity measur'd out to the proportion of each mind and spirit, each temper and disposition created so different each from other, and yet by the skill of wise conducting all to become uniform in vertue. To expedite these knots were worthy a learned and memorable Synod: while our enemies expect to see the expectation of the Church tir'd out with dependencies and independencies how they will compound, and in what Calends.

The hope that by such ideal considerations men might be persuaded to surrender the expectation of power is sufficient evidence of Milton's Utopian if noble impracticality. His ideas seem to have received no serious consideration. There was a wrangling *Answer*, and divorce came to be listed by men like Prynne, Pagitt, Baillie and Edwards with the other opprobrious errors of the time. Milton's argument was but a special phase of the issue of freedom and toleration.[66] What chiefly came of it at the moment was that Milton was driven to defend his right to free publication. The Assembly made a formal complaint to Parliament, on August 9, against the spread of heresy. Thomas Hill and Herbert Palmer preached before Parliament against toleration on August 13, and the latter publicly damned Milton's pamphlet. The Stationers' Company petitioned, on August 24, for stricter enforcement of the printing ordinance, and named as special offenders Milton and the unknown author of Overton's *Mans Mortallitie*.[67] Nothing came of these proceedings, the zealots being overawed, it would seem, by Cromwell, but the threat moved

[66] See Appendix B.   [67] See below, p. 96.

Milton to address Parliament again, this time for the liberty of unlicensed printing.

Areopagitica (November 24), 1644, takes its place as the most perfect literary expression of the ideal of freedom produced during the struggle of 1644. It was far from being the earliest or the most influential statement of the principle of toleration. The book went through but one edition. Whereas in contemporary pamphlets such works as *The Compassionate Samaritane, The Bloudy Tenent* and *Theomachia* are mentioned again and again in text or margin, Milton's tract seems to have roused no echo of condemnation or applause.[68] One can, however, easily believe that it was read with approval by Henry Lawrence. Milton addressed a sonnet to his son. He served later as President of the Council of State. He also wrote *Of our Communion and Warre with Angels* (May 8) 1646, a work which, somewhat in the spirit of *Areopagitica*, pictures the life of the soul as an inner war of good and evil. But to the pamphlet-reading public, at least until 1649, Milton was little known save as the writer of the divorce tracts. The reason for the neglect of *Areopagitica* is not far to seek. Agitation for freedom of the press as for toleration secured attention according to the practical importance of the cause it was expected to serve. Milton, free lance scholar, thinker, poet and prophet, little known outside the circle of a few friends, represented only Milton. *Areopagitica* dazzles with the vision of an England of free souls, kept bent to serve their maker by the ceaseless effort of poets and teachers. Government in such an England would foster the freedom of such men to pursue their function of combating error with their own weapons in their own way. For the moral life is a struggle endlessly renewed, and true freedom a call to battle for victory always remaining to be won in the soul. In the tooth-and-nail struggle of Presbyterians, Independents, Separatists and incipient Levellers, such notions naturally made no stir. Milton wrote not a pamphlet but a poem.

[68] See Appendix B.

X

TOLERATION, THE GREAT DIANA

JOHN LILBURNE

A Copie of a Letter to Mr. William Prinne Esq.[69]

The year 1644 was a critical point in the Puritan Revolution. The Presbyterian party was, so to speak, forced to go to the country with its proposal for the parochial regimentation of society. The opposition this provoked did more than give an airing to the case for toleration. It brought to view and for a time united the confused forces of individualism against revival in any form of the old type of church-state. Independents and sectaries drew together for self-defense against persecution, and found themselves on the same side with liberals and levellers of all kinds. They were not able to win Parliament or Assembly, but they developed an art of propaganda which enabled them more than to hold their own in the press, and the intransigence of their opponents gave the army into their hands. The inevitable result was the attempted establishment of a revolutionary state, doomed to go down in the failure of its leaders to hold the revolutionary elements of the population united, once the menace of religious persecution was removed.

If the history of ideas and their expression after 1644 were to be discussed and illustrated in full, it would have to follow along the several lines that led to the final repudiation of the Levellers by the Council of State in 1650. After that crucial disruption, it would trace the failure of the saints to rule alone, the dissipation of popular dissent in renewed sectarian activity, the premature imperialism by which Cromwell attempted to save the situation, and the ultimate return of

[69] Vol. III, p. 179.

monarchy on an artfully contrived wave of royalist sentiment. The limitations of space do not permit such treatment of the subject here. We shall content ourselves merely with indicating certain of the main lines of development in the literature of the revolution, and devote our chief attention to the Levellers. Lilburne's name has been sunk in misunderstanding and contempt, Walwyn's in oblivion, but the attempt of those men and their associates to turn the tide of the Puritan Revolution directly toward the establishment of democracy was fraught with greater meaning and interest for modern times than has commonly been realized.

While the war over toleration raged among the pamphleteers, the Presbyterian party endeavored to effect its own ends by legislation. The payment of tithes, assured to the clergy by ordinance in 1644, became the subject of bitter controversy and repeated Parliamentary enactment. The ordinance for ordination of the clergy, adopted in August, 1644, and revised in 1646, was accompanied by efforts to forbid lay preaching by law. In January, 1645, the Assembly, overriding the opposition of the Apologists, secured approval for its Directory setting up Presbyterian forms of public worship, though formal adoption by Parliament of the complete Presbyterian system did not come until August, 1648. The most desperate measure of the Presbyterians was, however, the ordinance introduced September 2, 1646, and adopted May 2, 1648, against blasphemy and heresy. This could be interpreted only as a threat to brand, maim or kill any who dared oppose them. It might, of course, have been the prelude to a period of actual terrorism had not the mounting successes of the New Model, justifying toleration as a war measure, rendered all Presbyterian enactments largely nugatory in effect.

The victories of the army of sectaries led by Fairfax and Cromwell emboldened dissent and drove the Presbyterians to apply themselves more hotly than ever to battle in the press. For the most part, they were slow to learn from their enemies the new tactics of popular polemics. Daniel Featley expressed the attitude of many of them in his Καταβάπτισται Κατάπτυστοι *Dippers Dipt. Or, the Anabaptists duck'd and plung'd Over Head and Eares* (February 7), 1645:

> With these Heretiques I enter into Lists in the ensuing Tractate, and without any flourish of Rhetorick at all fall upon them with Logicall and Theologicall weapons, wielded after a Scholasticall manner. . . . It is not beauty, and gorgeous apparell, but strength and valour, and *Armour of proof* makes a Warriour. . . . Pickt phrases and oranaments of Rhetorick and witty conceits doe well in Panegyricks, & Paraeneticks, but they are of little or no use in Polemicks. [*Epistle*]

With these sentiments, the style of the great pundits of Presbyterianism was in substantial accord. Baillie, Henderson and Gillespie went on vainly thundering down texts from their Scotch Sinai upon the heads of English heretics, and their English coadjutors followed suit as best they could.[70]

Prynne on the other hand had a method all his own, better fitted in some ways to the situation. Taking advantage of his influence with Parliament and bending every effort to crush his opponents, he poured forth the sweepings of his amazing mind in *Truth Triumphing over Falsehood* (January 2), 1645, *A Fresh Discovery of some Prodigious New Wandring-Blasing-Stars, & Firebrands* (July 24), 1645, *The Lyar Confounded* (October 15), and other tracts too numerous to mention. His terror rose to its highest pitch in *The Sword of Christian Magistracy* (March 9), 1647. He there draws from Deuteronomy the infallible precept that any who try to win people to new ways should die:

> even [if] any mans own natural brother, son, daughter, wife, nighest bosome and most endeared friend, which is his own soul, should entice him secretly to go and serve other gods (or the true God in a new and false manner) which he and his fathers had not known; . . . he SHAL

---

[70] Henderson, *A Sermon . . . before the House of Lords* (May 28), 1645; Gillespie, *A Sermon . . . before . . . the House of Lords* (August 27), 1645; Baillie, *Errours and Induration* (July 30), 1645, *A Dissuasive from the Errours of the Time* (November 24), second edition (January 22), 1646, *Anabaptism, the true Fountaine of Independency* (December 28), 1646; Rutherford, *A Survey of the Spiritual Antichrist* (November), 1647.

SURELY KIL THEM (without mercy) and his own hand shal be first upon them to put them to death; and afterwards the hands of all the people, and they shal stone them with stones that they dye; not because they actually seduced him or others; but because they sought to thrust him away from the Lord his God. [*Sword*, 5-6]

Panic could hardly go farther; yet Prynne's fear was real, and its cause not unintelligible. The torture, shame and danger which had been so dramatically reversed in his case to triumph and public honor had intensified a self-conceit already exaggerated almost to disease. It was as though ever afterwards the slightest disagreement set his ears tingling again. The pillory had privileged him to go undisputed. Martyrdom was his daily bread, and contradiction a scaffold on which to exhibit himself again a victim. His scars made him insensible to argument. Objections were the evidence of their authors' wickedness. The bitterest, the most damaging things that Robinson, Lilburne and Overton could say against him and his cause, he printed in his own *Fresh Discovery*. Nothing was said in his discredit which he would not scream again from the housetops as sufficient proof of the error and iniquity of all who opposed him. Whatever else he put into those pamphlets of his served merely to give further support to his pathological vanity. The thousands of precedents which he dragged by the ears from all the ages merely gave added assurance to his tortured pride that the law was and its strong arm ought to be on the side of him who had suffered under Archbishop Laud.

As the rage of Prynne shows, the state of mind of the Presbyterians was changing with the growing realization that success was slipping from them. With that came too the realization that their arguments were of little avail against the unscrupulous rhetoric of their antagonists. John Vicars observed in his *Picture of Independency* (March 15), 1645, that it was idle for him to "perplex his thoughts about the *Dogmaticall discussion* of the *Controversie*"; better "to look into the *practicall-manner* of managing the *matter* . . . on our *Dissent-*

ing-Brethrens part." He proceeds to make a vigorous attack not on the doctrine and logic but on the motives and the personal character of John Goodwin and Lilburne. In *The Schismatick Sifted* (June 22), 1646, he went on to show how the Independents and sectaries, by their holy lives, by their glozing piety of conversation, by their prating of new light and of charity and liberty, insinuated their poison into men's minds. John Bastwick, beginning mildly enough in *Independency not Gods Ordinance* (May 21), 1645, revived his old virtuosity in vituperation in a second part of that work (June 10), and in a *Just Defence* (August 30) combated Lilburne by putting in a discreditable light the latter's connection with his own *Letany* of former years. He also made general war on sectaries in *The Storming of the Anabaptists Garrisons* April 27), 1647. In *Heresiography* (May 8, 1645), Ephraim Pagitt abandoned argument altogether, and appealed to naked prejudice by merely listing heresies with exclamations of horror.

But the man who outdid all others in what Vicars called the practical rather than the dogmatical way of writing was Thomas Edwards. Edwards did not sit in his study dredging for texts with which to smite the heretics. He made it his business to read, if with starting eyes, the flood of heretical and seditious literature as it poured from the press. From this, from his own observation, from acquaintances and correspondents, he collected nearly three hundred dangerous opinions of the time, and heaped about them a prodigious assortment of distorted and libelous information concerning those who espoused them. All this he issued in the three amorphous parts, over six hundred pages in all, of his *Gangraena: Or a Catalogue and Discovery of many of the Errours, Heresies, Blasphemies, and Pernicious Practices of the Sectaries of this time* (I, February 26; II, May 28; III, December 28, 1646). He sacrificed every canon of logic, of good taste and, as John Goodwin pointed out, even of syntax, in the effort to make his readers realize what was happening about them. He mentioned names, dates and places, "bringing upon the stage matters of fact." "Such discoveries as these are a more sensible practicall way of confutation of the Sectaries to the body of the people of the Kingdome, then so many syllogismes and arguments; they can understand these when they cannot perceive an argument." [71] The effect of this method may perhaps be measured by the fact that its author was visited with the full weight of Goodwin in refutation,[72] that he succeeded in smoking Walwyn out of his anonymity,[73] and that he achieved the immortality of mention in a sonnet of Milton's (*On the New Forcers of Conscience*). A host of lesser pens helped to make his name a byword for bigotry run mad.

The man did indeed live in what seems to us a world of inverted ideas, but it was the only world he knew, and he saw it being turned upon its head. Though he writes, therefore, in a kind of vertigo, he nevertheless sees and expresses more vividly than do less hysterical writers the actual color of the time. Beyond Goodwin and the Independents, he sees wild sectaries like Saltmarsh, and beyond them the free thinkers, loose livers and levellers like Walwyn, Lilburne and Overton. He sees that there is no real Independent party but a mob of misbelievers with consciences which however tender will like the ostrich's stomach swallow anything. "Independencie and Sectarism in England" have become "but a politick State Faction, severing and dividing it self upon other private interests from the publike interest of this Church and State." Not only the conscientious dissenter but the ungodly of all sorts, "needy, broken decaied men," "guilty, suspicious and obnoxious men," "ambitious, proud, covetous men," "Libertines and loose persons," "all Wanton-witted, unstable, erroneous spirits," all those "discontented at the faithfull preaching of their Ministers close to their consciences," all such fly to Independency as to a sanctuary and cry for toleration as their great Diana (II, 183). Edwards does not spare particulars, and he

[71] *Gangraena* II, "To the Christian Reader."
[72] *Cretensis*, March 19, 1646.   [73] See below, pp. 108-110.

has a real gift for hitting off the characters of his enemies. There is "Goliah" Goodwin — "a man who seeks great swelling words of vanity." There is Walwyn — "a Seeker, and a dangerous man, a strong head." Lilburne is the "darling of the Sectaries," Overton "a desperate Sectary, one of Lilburnes Breed." Unscrupulous as he was in personal abuse, Edwards had a vision of the end toward which such men were leading. The old morality, the old discipline, the church and the social order, would all dissolve in the liberty of men to do as their lusts desired, in free thinking and democracy. It was as though modern society had been revealed to him in a witch's nightmare, and he had awakened with mind unhinged.

Not without reason did Edwards call Goodwin a Goliah, for the latter was easily the intellectual giant of the radical religious groups. He was holding the fort of debate until the moment should arrive for Pride's Purge, and his influence drilled and stiffened the forces of opinion behind the lines of the New Model. Though ejected from his church in May, 1645, he nevertheless organized about himself in the same street a kind of junta of earnest disciples. His enemies dubbed him the "busie bishop," the "monstrous Metropolitan of Coleman-Street Conclave." [74] John Bachiler licensed and Henry Overton sold the books which Matthew Simmons printed for him in cleaner fairer type on stronger whiter paper than were deemed worthy of all but the greatest rabbis of the day. In *Innocency and Truth Triumphing* (January 8), 1645, and *Calumny Arraign'd and Cast* (January 31), he made war upon Prynne. [75] In 1646, he reiterated his caveat against uniformity in *Twelve Considerable Serious Cautions* (February 17), and went into battle against Edwards in *Cretensis* (March

[74] See *A Testimony to the Truth of Jesus Christ . . . Subscribed by the Ministers of Jesus Christ within the Province of London* (December 14, 1647); Goodwin, *Sion-Colledg Visited* (February 1, 1648); William Jenkyn, Ἀλλοτριοεπίσκοπος, *The Busie Bishop* (March 30); Goodwin, Νεοφυτο πρεσβύτερος; or the *Yongling Elder* (June 15); Jenkyn, Ὁδηγος Τοφλος, *The Blinde Guide* (June 15); also John Vicars, *Coleman-street Conclave Visited* (March 21), with a satirical portrait of Goodwin (see frontispiece *Volume* II).

[75] See above, p. 53.

19) and *Anapologesiates Antapologias* (August 27). When in the same year the heresy ordinance was introduced, he promptly responded with *Some Modest and Humble Queries* (September 22), which he defended at length in *Hagiomastix* (February 5), 1647. The intricate dialectic of the latter called for further exposition in *A Candle to See the Sunne* (February 18) and *A Postscript or Appendix* (April 2). In *The Divine Authority of the Scriptures* (December 18), assailing clerical pretensions to infallibility, he went dangerously close to defending a rational view-point in biblical criticism, and he pursued the Presbyterian divines to their lair in *Sion-Colledg Visited* (February 1), 1648. Finally, with *Right and Might Well Met* (January 2), 1649, he came triumphant to the support of the army's forcible seizure of power.

Goodwin's service to the revolutionary cause in the mêlée of pulpit and press was primarily that he could give better than he got in battle with the theological technicians. He never flagged in expounding the Scripture and logic of congregationalism, and when the need arrived, he transposed the principle of *salus populi suprema lex*, which he had used to justify popular uprising against the king, to justify as well the action of the army against Parliament. Arguing as he was for his own personal safety against the threat of the heresy ordinance, he readily embraced the conviction that God gave authority to rule to that power which would keep safe the liberty of Independent ministers and their congregations to debate endlessly the points of faith and the nature of truth. For it was not, after all, the political but the intellectual struggle that commanded Goodwin's full interest. The liberty of churches was essential that he might be free to speculate and preach. Beyond that he had no constructive ideas, and when safety was afforded him after 1649, he devoted himself to exhaustive polemic for the doctrine of free will.

The most attractive of all Goodwin's writings is that on *The Divine Authority of Scriptures*. He there ventures to deny the literal authority of the Bible, and to argue that the written word in original or translation depends for acceptance on the appeal of style and essential reasonableness to the individual intelligence. "The true and proper *foundation of Christian Religion* is not ink and paper, not any book or books, not any writing, or writings whatsoever, whether *Translations* or *Originalls*; but that substance of matter, those gracious counsells of God concerning the salvation of the world by Jesus Christ." [76] Cast in other circumstances, the writer of these words might have found his place among the Cambridge Platonists, as certain fundamental resemblances of thought, if not of temper, to Cudworth's sermon of the same year suggest. [77] As it was, his subtle and eloquent idealism served to give force and glamor to the desperate effort for mere survival on the part of congregations of Puritan saints, men who would stop far short in practice of the ideal liberty which Goodwin reached after in speculation. Walwyn gives what is probably an accurate indication of the effect upon tougher minds of all that flow of reasoning: "My character of him usually was that he spent much time (in my apprehension) to make plain things difficult to be understood, and then labour'd again to make them plain and easie to be understood; but he had so perplex'd them, as that he could not." [78]

Of the cloud of Independent and sectarian preachers and writers to whom Goodwin was so freely accused of giving countenance, only a few can be mentioned here. The practical usefulness of toleration as a military and political policy was expressed by Hugh Peters with racy vigor in *Mr. Peters Last Report of the English Wars* (August 27), 1646. In William Dell's *Power from on High, Or the Power of the Holy Ghost* (May 8), 1645, one may still be moved by the fiery words in

[76] *Divine Authority*, 17.

[77] Ralph Cudworth, *Sermon . . . before the . . . House of Commons* (March 31), 1647 (Reprinted by the Facsimile Text Society, 1930): "Inke and paper can never make us Christians, can never beget a new nature, a living principle in us; can never form Christ or any true notion of spiritual things in our hearts. The Gospel, that new Law which Christ delivered to the world, is not merely a *Letter* without us, but a *quickening* spirit within us" (p. 5).

[78] *Just Defence*, 29.

which for the benefit of the New Model the doctrine of free conscience and the indwelling spirit was translated into the will to victory. Samuel Richardson put with incisiveness *Certain Questions propounded to the Assembly whether corporall punishments may be inflicted upon such as hold Errours in Religion* (December 10), 1646.[79] John Saltmarsh provided the more enthusiastic sects with an expression which was not mere mystical jargon of their dream of universal love. Part whirling dervish, Saltmarsh was also part pure poet and saint of God. His *Dawnings of Light* (January 4), 1645, *Smoke in the Temple* (January 16), 1646, *Groanes for Liberty* (March 10), *Reasons for Unitie* (June 17) and *Sparkles of Glory* (May 27), 1647, touched as they are now and then with genuine beauty of language, still convey something of their author's vision of that fraternity of the spirit which alone heals divisions and concludes debates. In his last moments, with the hand of death upon him, the man went to Fairfax and Cromwell themselves with a true flash of prophetic warning.[80]

Saltmarsh was really giving premonition of that last and final wave of revolution which was to spend itself in the Quakers. The immediate practical effect to which Goodwin's idealism led appeared rather in the part played by John Price, William Kiffen and their like. These were solid, steady men of the authentic nonconformist type, pillars of the conventicle and of the market place. They worked in more or less uncomfortable alliance with Walwyn, Lilburne and the Levellers until the triumph of the army over Parliament removed the menace of the heresy ordinance. They then accepted the measure of toleration calculated for the meridian of Cromwellian England by John Owen. Jeremy Taylor among others had by that time clearly limited the definition of heresy to sedition against the state.[81] Owen's position was that "if *Opinions* in

[79] Reiterated in *Fifty Questions* (May 21), 1647, and in *The Necessity of Toleration* (September 17).
[80] *Wonderful Predictions* (December 29), 1647.
[81] Θεολογία 'Εκλεκτική. *A Discourse of the Liberty of Prophesying* (June 28), 1647.

their owne nature tend to the disturbance of the *publike peace*, either that *publike Tranquillitie* is not of God, or God alloweth a penall restraint of these Opinions." The day after the execution of Charles, he preached a sermon to this effect before the members of the Rump Parliament,[82] and we can be sure that the men who listened to his words were troubled by no doubts concerning the divine origin of the peace which had just been made by the sword. Neither did the makers of that peace doubt that God intended the opinions of English Protestants, including Presbyterians, Independents and the recognized sects, to be free from penal restraints. All others must beware lest in their own nature they tend to disturb the peace. This became the working principle of the Cromwellian attempt to settle the question of church government, and its author became first Cromwell's chaplain in Ireland and then Vice-chancellor of the University of Oxford. With that settlement, the Independent and Baptist leaders were in the main to prove satisfied, though Goodwin himself characteristically protested against the interference of Cromwell's Triers with congregational freedom.[83] When, therefore, the Levellers made their last stand in 1649 for the consummation of the revolution by measures anticipating the reforms of the nineteenth century, Goodwin's associates repudiated their former allies, particularly Walwyn, not only as disturbers of the state but also as enemies of religion.[84]

The Levellers indeed, alone among the contending groups of the time, were not a church or a sect but a party. If they joined with the Independents and the sects to oppose

[82] *Sermon . . . With a Discourse about Toleration* (January 31), 1649. The quotation given above is from the *Discourse*, p. 41. See also Οὐρανῶν Οὐρανία. *The Shaking and Translating of Heaven and Earth* (April 19).

[83] Βασανιστάι, *Or the Triers (or Tormentors)* (May 23), 1657.

[84] Kiffen and others, *The Petition of Several Churches . . . called Anabaptists* (April 2), 1649, disavowed approval of Lilburne's *Englands New Chains*, which appears to have been previously submitted to them for signature, and to have been read in some of their meetings. See also Lilburne, Walwyn, Prince and Overton, *A Manifestation* (April 14); Kiffen, Price and others, *Walwins Wiles* (May 10); Brooke, *The Charity of Church-men* (May 28); Walwyn, *The Fountain of Slander* (May 30), and *Walwyns Just Defence*, 1649.

persecution, it was not because they desired as a group to propagate any particular religious faith or to establish any special form of religious organization. Their methods and objects were political and secular, and this doubtless was the secret of their undoing. Cromwell and the army leaders after 1649 were prepared to grant a measure of religious toleration. But to the Levellers, the toleration of religious differences was but a step toward the establishment of a state in which not alone religious differences but political opposition — the expression of substantial grievances and of demands for concrete reforms having nothing to do with religion — should not only be tolerated but admitted to a legitimate place and function in government. This was for them but the practical inference to be drawn from the deadlock of dogmatisms and from the manifest fact that zeal against the heretic's error was generally animated by the desire to command his body and estate. But if religious persecution were but a cover for political and economic oppression, it followed that oppression might continue, and with it the natural need for self-defense, even under religious toleration. There could be no liberty without toleration, but toleration was not enough. For the protection of the individual and the restraint of privilege in all its forms, the Levellers therefore pressed in the name of natural right for the adoption of popular representative government under a fundamental law or agreement of the people. The proposal was momentous but premature. The men whom revolution had raised to power had minds which still moved in the formulas of church and religion. They could not conceive of a society or a form of government which intrusted the welfare of the people not to the godly, especially when providentially elected in battle, but to the people themselves, directed, it might be, by pamphleteers and demagogues. The saints of the congregations looked upon the Levellers as enemies of religion. Cromwell suppressed them as enemies of the state. Their interest for us is that they pointed clearly to the natural outcome of the struggle for religious liberty in the political and economic individualism of modern times, and that they attached to the cause of individualism those formulas and images of man and nature of which Europe was not soon to hear the last.

Only with ample reservations can we assert who was responsible for the inception of the Leveller point of view, and what were the circumstances under which the movement took its rise and ran its course. Its leaders were not clergymen or even tub preachers but for the most part men of yeoman stock, possessed of some education and engaged as a rule none too prosperously in trade. They appealed to others like themselves, to young men and apprentices, artisans and shopkeepers, the class quickest to feel the pinch of hard times. They were men given to attendance upon sermons, to the reading of pamphlets, and to much talk among themselves in their shops, on the streets, or at the tavern. Needy and discontented, they readily gravitated toward the sects and the army, but they were also ready to fall in behind anyone who could make use of the new arts and instruments of communication to call a crowd to his heels. The rapidity and success with which this was accomplished by the Levellers owed much to the conjunction, in 1645, of Lilburne and Walwyn, two men of contrasting but complementary qualities, with whom perhaps we should associate Richard Overton. The interest of historians has been so centered upon Charles and Cromwell, and upon all that they have come to represent in the later life of English-speaking peoples, that the first great democrats of modern times have until recently fallen far short of anything like due attention.

In the early months of 1645, the Independents, though they had not succeeded in getting their way with the church, had got their way with the army by means of the Self-denying Ordinance. The Presbyterians on the other hand were left to confront in heightened alarm charges of corrupt and treasonable practices on the part of their leaders in Parliament. At the same time, the clamor for toleration steadily mounted

as the New Model moved on to Naseby (June 14). Under
these conditions, Prynne addressed himself through the Parliamentary Committee for Examinations to support of the
Stationers' Company in its effort to enforce the printing ordinance. Two of the worst offenders, Goodwin and Saltmarsh,
were, to be sure, shielded by the imprimatur of John Bachiler,
but their respective booksellers, Henry Overton and Giles Calvert, could be made objects of attack. At Overton's shop, it
was alleged, all kinds of books against the Presbyterians were
sold "and 'tis given out the man sels them, but not the Master." [85] How large was the circulation of such publications
would be difficult to say, but they probably passed from hand
to hand in considerable numbers. Edwards asserts that Lilburne's pamphlets, "being unlicensed and of such kinde of
Arguments, sell dear." [86] On the other hand, we know that
the penny pamphlet printed on one sheet (eight pages) was
common. Prynne says that Lilburne paid for the printing of
his attacks on Colonel King, and took two hundred copies
for circulation among his friends.[87] Goodwin's congregation
is reported to have contributed fifty shillings toward the printing of ten thousand copies of Walwyn's *Word in Season*, some
of which were handed about in Westminster Hall by Lilburne
himself.[88] Henry Robinson, we have seen, was accused by
Prynne of having his own press and summoned before the
Committee of Examinations.[89] Though not himself one of
them, he was familiarly known to the Levellers, and the
committee summoned Lilburne and Jane Coe on the same
occasion. The latter, successor to Andrew Coe, her husband, and proprietor of a press which did a large business of
the cheaper sort, was no doubt none too scrupulous in observ-
ing the printing ordinance, but nothing was proved against
her at this time. Some connection, however, may have existed
between her shop and Thomas Paine, a printer in the same

[85] Edwards, *Gangraena*, II, 9.   [86] *Gangraena*, I, 96.
[87] *Lyar Confounded*, 4.
[88] Thomason's note to *Word in Season* (May 26) ; *Walwyns Just Defence*, 31.
[89] *Fresh Discovery*, 10.

neighborhood of Cripplegate, who shortly before had been associated with Matthew Simmons, printer for Henry Overton. Paine, on his own account, printed many of Walwyn's tracts and may have had a hand in other work for the Levellers.

The men immediately associated with Lilburne had in the meantime set up a printing press of their own, which seems to have been operated chiefly by William Larner and Richard Overton, and which, harried by the agents of the Stationers' Company, was moved from time to time from one place to another. From it were issued in all probability the pamphlets which came in 1645 and the first half of 1646 from Lilburne, Overton, Larner and other members of the fast growing radical group. By the summer of 1646, the three men mainly concerned were in prison and their press broken up, but this did not prevent them or their adherents from promptly securing the use of other presses for the publication of the pamphlets which continued to flow from their pens.[90]

The reappearance of John Lilburne in London in January 1645 provided the Presbyterians with a new and formidable antagonist, and the cause of popular liberty with a daring and picturesque hero and spokesman. Lilburne had led an exciting career since his release from prison by Parliament in 1640. Enlisting in Lord Brooke's regiment, he had been captured and exchanged by the Royalists, and his gallantry had won him a lieutenant-colonelcy. He had also won the esteem of Cromwell, who was now depending on him to serve as a witness to the charges against Manchester which preluded the Self-denying Ordinance and the New Model. But Lilburne also smarted under grievances of his own. Somehow linked in

[90] H. R. Plomer, *Secret Printing During the Civil War* in "The Library," Vol. V (Second Series), London, 1904. A comprehensive study of the operations of the press and the book trade during the civil wars and the Commonwealth would be of great interest and value. So great is the difficulty of identifying the work of the many cheap and illicit presses of the period that the statements made above should be taken with some caution. Plomer's article, valuable as it is, remains incomplete and, though accurate as far as it goes, is not wholly convincing in its inferences.

his mind with the alleged treason of Manchester was the personal wrong done him by his former commander, Colonel King. Parliament had not settled, and with Prynne to the fore did not bid fair soon to settle, the claims due on account of his former illegal imprisonment. As the debate over the New Model waxed fierce, it became clear that he could not retain his place in the army unless he would take the Covenant, which his conscience loathed. At the same time, the privileges which had been granted to the Merchant Adventurers barred him from the wool trade. And to cap all, the Assembly was attempting to dictate his religion, the Stationers were attempting to deny him the freedom of the press, and his old fellow sufferer, Prynne, was hounding the Independents and sectaries, who were fighting Parliament's battles. In *A Copie of a Letter . . . to Mr. William Prinne Esq.* (dated by the author January 7, and by Thomason January 15), Lilburne at once issued a public defiance which gave perfect expression to his genius for dramatic identification of his own cause and personality with the cause of popular freedom. Speaking of himself and Prynne, he says, "The eyes of the people of God are therefore the more upon us, and are subject with lesse jealousie to receive those things that come from us for truth." He turns to immediate histrionic account the scornful comparison made by a friend of Prynne's: "Goe you, and tell the tall Cedar, the little Shrub will have a bout with him." The bout proposed was a public debate on the question of toleration.

XI

TOLERATION AND LAISSEZ FAIRE

[WILLIAM WALWYN]

*A Helpe to the right understanding of a Discourse
concerning Independency* [91]

Prynne did not accept Lilburne's challenge to debate toleration, but at once sought means to silence its proposer. Lilburne
had to appear several times, though without result, before the
Committee for Examinations.[92] Then on July 19, pretext was
found for putting him once more under arrest. The occasion
was provided by the appearance at the doors of the House of
Commons of William Walwyn and a committee of citizens
seeking to present charges against the Speaker of the House.

Walwyn had had up to this time, it would seem, little or no
acquaintance with Lilburne. After his efforts of the preceding
year on behalf of the Baptists, evidenced in *The Compassionate Samaritane*, he had, however, been moving about according to his wont among the people, continuing especially
to seek out those who were being subjected to persecution of
any kind.[93] He was also actively engaged in the organization
of protests to Parliament in the popular interest. By his own
account he took part in the meeting at which two or three
hundred citizens, Lilburne being prominent among them,

[91] Vol. III, p. 189.

[92] Lilburne, *Reasons*; Prynne, *Lyar Confounded*.

[93] Walwyn's *Helpe* was written in large measure to defend John Goodwin.
Other evidence of Walwyn's endeavor to play the part of compassionate
Samaritan may be seen a little later in *The Afflicted Christian justifyed. In a
Letter to Mr. Thomas Hawes An honest and Godly Man, and known friend
to his country, Now Prisoner for supposed Blasphemy* . . . (May 18), 1646.
This letter bears many signs of having come from Walwyn. See also Hawes'
Christian Relation (March 31, 1646). Style, point of view and the imprint of
Thomas Paine also suggest that Walwyn came to the support of the citizens
of Norwich in their resistance to persecution in *Vox Populi, or the Peoples
Cry against the Clergy* (August 25), 1646.

gathered at the Windmill Tavern directly after the loss of Leicester (May 31).[94] This meeting angered the Presbyterians by proposing to Parliament that members of the Assembly be sent down to the country to incite the people further to resist the king. He had also been taking part in certain other meetings of citizens at Salter's Hall.[95] They had set about investigating among other matters acts of Speaker Lenthall and his brother, which they suspected were treasonable to the Parliamentary cause. On July 19, they sent a committee which included Walwyn to present their information to the House of Commons, and there, while waiting at the door of the house, they found John Lilburne also in attendance about business of his own.

Meanwhile Walwyn had not been neglecting to deal in his own way with Prynne in the press. The result of his activity is to be found in a little pamphlet which gives interesting evidence of its author's steady advance in the art of propaganda and in the clarification of his understanding of essential principles at stake. Prynne's *Independency Examined* (September 26), 1644, like his other tracts, had been published with a somewhat larger page than was customary and with a distinctive title-page. Walwyn issued his brief reply in almost precisely similar form. The title, *A Helpe to the right understanding of a Discourse concerning Independency. Lately published by William Pryn of Lincolns Inne, Esquire* (February 6), 1645, was so couched and so arranged upon the page as to suggest to the reader that this was another work by Prynne himself. The intention, at any rate, was, on behalf of the Independents and Separatists, particularly of John Goodwin, to appeal to love and reason even in readers and followers of Prynne. Prynne is described as one who has suffered in the public cause but who, misled perhaps by defective understanding, has himself now turned to the persecution of others in the pursuit of his own interest. The man is a lawyer, and Walwyn distrusts lawyers as he has distrusted clergymen.

[94] *Whisper*, 4, 6.　　[95] *Ibid.*, 4, 6.

Thus Walwyn comes to a restatement of his former plea for
the toleration of religious dissenters, from whom he is again
at pains to dissociate himself in his own beliefs and practices.
Toleration, however, is now clearly but the condition for that
larger liberty which is the sole basis of public good. Let government merely maintain public peace, and leave every man to
the guidance of his own judgment in all things possible. Then
all things will flourish in the commonwealth. With this premonition of the doctrine of laissez faire, Walwyn was ripe
for sharing with Lilburne the leadership of a movement for
the establishment of political democracy.

XII

THE UNREASON OF PERSECUTION

[RICHARD OVERTON]

The Araignement of Mr. Persecution [96]

Richard Overton was perhaps, among all the supporters of Lilburne in 1645, the most outspoken and violent. He was, as we have seen, actively engaged at the moment in the printing of pamphlets in Lilburne's cause, but he was something more than a printer. Little is known of his previous career except that he seems to have been at one time in Holland and Germany. He was, it is likely, a kinsman of Henry Overton. In 1642, he had printed some verse satires of his own composition against the prelates, *Articles of high Treason . . . against Cheap-side Crosse* (January) and *New Lambeth Fayre* (March). He perhaps first revived the name and fame of Martin Marprelate [97] by republishing *The Character of a Puritan* (January 31), 1643. Shortly afterwards, he published a work which throws interesting light on the speculative background of the democratic movement. The seventeenth-century approach to rationalism was through a theology which sought to resolve religion into a purely natural phenomenon,

[96] Vol. III, p. 203.

[97] The appearance of numerous pamphlets in the reign of Elizabeth, written in the interest of the Presbyterian party in the Church, led to the Star-Chamber decree of 1586, forbidding any publication without permission of the Archbishop of Canterbury or the Bishop of London. This was the occasion for an outburst in the illicit press of popular indignation at the bishops. In 1588-1589, appeared a series of witty and vivacious tracts, couched somewhat as dramatic monologues, and covering the bishops with ridicule. The author or authors, who may have been John Penry and Job Throckmorton, either or both, wrote over the pseudonym, Martin Marprelate. They also made use of the names Martin Senior and Martin Junior, sons to the original Martin. There were numerous imitations of the Mar-prelate tracts. *Hay any Worke for Cooper* was republished in (March) 1642, and the pseudo-Martin's *Dialogue*, with the title *Character of a Puritan*, in (January 31), 1643.

establish natural reason as a sufficient basis for knowing God, and make of the supernatural at most merely a far off divine event. Overton, falling in some fashion under the influence of Socinus, essayed a statement of these ideas in *Mans Mortallitie or a Treatise Wherein 'tis proved, both Theologically and Phylosophically, that whole Man, (as a rationall Creature) is a Compound wholly mortall, contrary to that common distinction of Soule and Body* (January 19), 1644; (later editions 1644, 1655). With characteristic clarity and positive tone, Overton asserts that the soul, one with the body, is subject to the same laws of procreation, growth and death. To these laws, Christ subjected himself and, by natural kinship with the son of man, all men share in the resurrection of soul and body and, unless they have rejected Christ, in his atonement for sin. Similar views appear in Milton, and Overton's pamphlet was indeed condemned by the Stationers' Remonstrance [98] along with the *Doctrine and Discipline of Divorce.* Nevertheless, when Overton was seized by the Council of State in 1649, the soldiers took from him "certain papers which were my former Meditations upon the works of Creation, intituled, *Gods Word confirmed by his Works*; wherein I endeavoured the probation of a *God*, a *Creation*, a *State of Innocencie*, a *Fall*, a *Resurrection*, a *Restorer*, a *Day of Judgment*, &c. barely from the consideration of *things visible and created*: and these papers I preserved to perfect and publish as soon as I could have any rest from the turmoils of this troubled Common-wealth." [99]

[98] See above, p. 74.
[99] *Picture of the Councel of State* (April 11), 1649, 28. Edwards, *Gangraena*, I, 81-82, II, 17-18, asserts that Overton's notions were the heresy of a group of Anabaptists, among whom he names Overton and, as the principal author of the pamphlet, Clement Wrighter. In each edition of the work, however, the author is said to be, "R. O.", and the identification of these initials with Overton is supported by an allusion in the latter's *Araignement of Mr. Persecution*, 20. The matter has been discussed by Saurat, *Milton Man and Thinker*, 310-322, who thinks that Milton collaborated in the revised edition of *Mans Mortallitie*, which appeared in 1655 under the title *Man Wholly Mortal*. That Milton gave to the "mortallist" heresy an important place in his own doctrine is well known. The evidence that he had any hand in the pamphlet is unconvincing.

For speculations on natural religion, Overton could indeed find little leisure in the turmoil of 1645, but he could turn his pen to the fiery proclamation of its dogmas. No writer of the time went further than he in the assertion of the natural supremacy of reason even in matters of religion. From this basic principle were derived in his mind the natural freedom of all men in the exercise of reason and the natural equality of human rights. Persecution, therefore, was the unforgivable sin against the religion of nature, and on that ground he attacked the Presbyterians of Assembly and Parliament with boldness and imaginative power. *The Araignement of Mr. Persecution* (April 8), 1645, anticipating the allegorical methods of Bunyan,[100] turned to literary account the experience which popular agitators like Overton had been having with prosecutions in court. Mr. Persecution, defended by Sir Symon Synod and Sir John Presbyter, is prosecuted for treason by Mr. Gods-Vengance before Lord Parliament as judge. The jury includes such characters as Mr. Creation and Mr. Light-of-nature as well as Mr. Gospel, Mr. Good-samaritane (with reference to Walwyn's pamphlet), and Mr. Trueth-and-peace (with reference to Williams's *Bloudy Tenent*). Overton goes the full length of demanding toleration even for Jews, and though the doctrinal case for liberty of conscience is faithfully presented by Mr. Gospel, the most notable and to Overton's opponents the most objectionable feature of his tract was the trenchant presentation of the argument against religious uniformity on the rationalistic grounds of political advantage and natural right.

The Araignement of Mr. Persecution, published over the pseudonym, Martin Marpriest, and attributed by Prynne in *Fresh Discovery* to Henry Robinson, seems to have been issued by Overton's illicit press in numerous copies and in

---

For the difficulty of establishing any personal connection between Milton and the heretics and radicals of Overton's social rank, see Appendix B.

[100] The resemblance of Overton's allegory to the trial scene in Bunyan's *Holy War* has been pointed out by Pease in his *Leveller Movement*, 100 n. Compare also the trial of Faithful in *Pilgrim's Progress*.

several printings or editions. The true authorship was not generally known until Overton's own acknowledgment in a subsequent pamphlet, *Picture of the Council of State*, published in 1649. The work was, of course, the cause of great perturbation in the breasts of such men as Prynne,[101] Edwards,[102] and Vicars,[103] and the agents of the Stationers' Company quickened their efforts to apprehend the authors and printers of all such publications. Overton for his part, still masquerading as Martin Marpriest, continued to harry the Assembly in *A Sacred Decretall* (May 31), 1645, *Martins Eccho* (June 27), *The Nativity of Sir John Presbyter* (July 2), *The Ordinance for Tythes Dismounted* (December 29), and *Divine Observations* (January 24), 1646. Upon Lilburne's arrest and imprisonment in the following July, he was ready to argue even more directly and explicitly for the rights of man.

[101] *Fresh Discovery.*
[102] *Gangraena.*
[103] *Schismatick Sifted.*

XIII

THE TRIBUNE OF THE PEOPLE

[JOHN LILBURNE]

Englands Birth-Right Justified [104]

Lilburne's challenge to Prynne to a public debate on toleration [105] was not accepted, but it served to give notice that a
new and formidable antagonist had entered the lists against
the party in power in Parliament and Assembly. That party
had by this time engendered its place holders and profiteers
as well as its zealots, and all its elements recognized in Lilburne a dangerous antagonist. Prynne had him summoned
several times, though without avail, before the Committee for
Examinations. [106] Then on July 19, as we have seen, he happened to appear at Westminster just at the moment when
Walwyn and the committee from Salter's Hall were waiting
to present information against Speaker Lenthall and his
brother. Colonel King and Bastwick were also about. There
was talk between Lilburne and Walwyn, together with other
members of the latter's committee. This was attended by tale-
bearing of some sort to and by Bastwick. Nothing came of
the committee's charges against the Speaker, but Lilburne suddenly found himself under arrest by order of the House. He
was not, however, to be so easily silenced or discredited. He
had been countenanced by Cromwell, now the hero of Naseby.
He had learned the uses of publicity, and had tasted popular
acclaim. Men like Walwyn and the Salter's Hall committee
had, moreover, learned the methods and power of organization. From the prison to which Lilburne was sent, he promptly
put forth an account of the ill treatment he had received, [107] and

[104] Vol. III, p. 257.   [105] See above, p. 91.
[106] Lilburne, *Reasons*; Prynne, *Lyar Confounded*.
[107] *Copy of a Letter . . . to a Friend,* dated by the author July 25, by Thomason August 9.

Prynne and Bastwick themselves testify that his friends rallied
to his support.[108] On August 26, his adherents submitted —
and here Walwyn's hand may be suspected — a petition in his
behalf,[109] signed by two or three thousand persons. During
the remainder of his enforced leisure, which lasted until his
discharge, October 14, he prepared a long pronunciamento
called *Englands Birth-Right* (October 10). After his release,
he continued to press his claims for compensation for his old
Star-Chamber imprisonment and to prosecute his case against
Colonel King. He also pursued the larger quarrel in a reply to
Prynne, *Innocency and Truth* (January 6), 1646. Interesting
evidence appeared in May of the growing cohesion of his party
with the followers of John Goodwin. The Presbyterian clergy
had presented to the Assembly (January 1) *A Letter of the*

---

[108] *Lyar Confounded, Just Defence.*

[109] The sources of information concerning these incidents are *Commons Journal*, IV, 212 ff.; Lilburne, *Copy of a Letter to a Friend* (July 25); Bastwick, *Just Defence* (August 30); Prynne, *Lyar Confounded* (October 15); Lilburne, *Innocency and Truth* (January 6), 1646, *True Relation* (February 23), *Just Mans Justification* (June 6), and *Free-Mans Freedome* (June 16). The failure of Pease (*Leveller Movement*, 104-105) to connect Walwyn with the Salter's Hall Committee is no doubt due to the fact that the name is given by both Bastwick and Lilburne as "Worley" or "Worly." But Walwyn himself says (*Whisper*, 4) that he had been active in "all the proceedings of Salters Hall," and Lilburne's reference is to "one Mr. *Worly*, that lives about Moore Fields," where we know Walwyn to have lived (*Fountain*, 1, 2; *Charity of Churchmen*, 10). Bastwick, describing the Salter's Hall Committee as he saw its members waiting outside the doors of the House, says "to speake the truth, *Worly* was one of the prosperest Gentlemen amongst them all, by reason of his habit and busie diligence . . .; he was mighty diligent about the Common-wealth that day, and the Priviledges of the Subject, and all the fraternity came flocking about him upon all occasions, as a company of Turkyes doe about a Frogge; wondering at her as at a strange sight: Without doubt when the Parliament comes to be recruted, the Independents will make him a Member," (*Just Defence*, 17). The suspicion that the Independents wished to send Walwyn to Parliament is also voiced by Edwards (*Gangraena*, II, 29). Walwyn himself spelt his name as it commonly appears, but it was probably pronounced something like Wallin, as indeed Edwards wrote it (*Gangraena*, I, 44). In the clatter of a committee, it might easily have been heard as Worley. Walwyn and Lilburne may already have seen one another at the Windmill Tavern, but the inference is probable that their real acquaintance dated from the affair of the Salter's Hall Committee. Bastwick's description of "Worley" in his *Just Defence*, like Lilburne's reference in *Copy of a Letter to a Friend*, suggests that the writer had not known Walwyn previously. Lilburne again refers to "Worly" in *Innocency and Truth* (January 6), 1646, but after that always to Walwyn.

Ministers . . . against Toleration. This received prompt reply from Richard Overton in *Divine Observations* (January 24), and from Walwyn in *Tolleration Justified* (January 29). The latter was also ready with rejoinders to the first two parts of Edwards's *Gangraena* as they appeared. On May 26, after stormy scenes at Guildhall, the Common Council of the City of London sent to the House of Commons a *Humble Remonstrance and Petition* demanding the suppression of heresy, the enforcement of the Presbyterian Directory and peace with the king. This was vigorously challenged, probably by Overton or some other member of the Lilburne following, in *The Interest of England Maintained* (June 8), 1646, and by someone in John Goodwin's circle in a *Moderate Reply* (June 12). John Bellamie issued *A Vindication of the Remonstrance* (July 6), which was met in turn by John Price with *The City-Remonstrance Remonstrated* (July 24). But in the meantime even before the Remonstrance could be submitted to the House, Walwyn was ready to warn the public with *A Word in Season* (May 18). Significant of what had been going on among his associates was the fact that ten thousand copies of this pamphlet had been printed, partly at the expense of Goodwin's congregation, and that John Lilburne went about distributing them in Westminster Hall on the day the Remonstrance was presented.[110] Directly after this incident, embroiled once more with the House of Lords over the King affair, Lilburne was seized again and sent to Newgate, thence to be shifted presently to the Tower, and there to remain with an interval of liberty in 1647 until August, 1648. But Lilburne behind bars, as Overton made haste to depict him in the frontispiece to *A Remonstrance of Many Thousand* (July 7), was precisely what was needed to convert revolutionary sentiment into a coherent movement.

To trace in detail the development of that movement and of the thought of its leaders, is not here so important as to define with clarity the significance of Lilburne's career and

110 See above, p. 89.

personality. That the welfare of the people was the supreme obligation of the state, that the people were in the nature of things the final judge of their own welfare, that to serve and defend the people was a high religious duty, these were abstract propositions of which more than one party in the struggle had availed itself. Lilburne offered little essentially new in principle. What he did was to offer his own case as a test of principles which had been upon many lips. He was one of the people. What did government propose to do about his welfare? His egotism in thus thrusting himself upon the center of the stage was, of course, almost as egregious as that of Prynne himself, an egotism which every effort to silence merely aggravated and infuriated. But he served his ego by impersonating not Jehovah or Moses but the free-born Johns of England. His grievance was their grievance, and he would accept no redress which was not also theirs. Thus he made the whole meaning and purpose of the Revolution seem to be that he and they should get what they chose to call their rights. Justly might Prynne complain that "*poor upstart John* is lately swelled to such an Altitude of worth and Merit in his own conceite . . . that he thinks the whole Parliament guilty of a breach of *Magna Charta* for not setting all publike businesses aside, to heare his private Petition and give him Reparations." [111] This was precisely Lilburne's point. Parliament had nothing so important to do as to serve poor upstart John, and now John was in position to turn and to teach others to turn to *Magna Charta* for support. Prynne was credibly informed "that this *upstart monstrous Lawyer* since he was called to the Barre at *Newgate*, where he now practiceth, hath the *Book of Statutes* there lying open before him, which he reads and interprets to all the poore *ignorant people* that visit him." [112]

Lilburne appeared as defendant, appellant, attorney and reporter in his own case. Until the very end, his procedure in each appearance before committee or court was not to seek

[111] *Lyar Confounded*, 14.   [112] *Ibid.*, 22.

acquittal or escape but to defy the authority of those who sought to examine or try him contrary to his notion of law and right. Though in the early stages he appealed from the Peers to the Commons, he was quite ready to defy the Commons too on the same grounds. His appeal was in effect to no recognized tribunal or statute but always to the public and to the popular sense of justice. He denied that any law could be more than "a shell without a kernell, a shadow without substance, and a body without a soul," unless executed according to "equity and reason," and this could not be so long as the cries of the poor went unheard, their miseries disregarded, their freedom denied. No court should acquit Lilburne unless it did justice to the people, and unless it did justice, he would put his very judges on trial before the bar of the people's judgment.

In his realized power to accomplish just this, lay, perhaps, Lilburne's greatest significance. The defenders of Parliament had themselves alleged that the necessity of the people knew no law higher than itself, but they could conceive no means save Parliament by which the people might be said to judge of their necessity. Presbyterians and Independents alike admitted the compulsion of conscience but no corporate expression of conscience outside the church or congregation. So long as the people lacked means outside of Parliament and the church for learning one another's mind, for arriving in effective numbers at any common judgment or for taking common action, they remained in truth the beast of many heads. But conditions had now radically changed. The people were becoming an urban multitude. The printing press clattered in their midst, and no prohibition in the swarming streets and rookeries of London could be effectively enforced against it. In these circumstances, the doctrine of the higher law assumed new and greater practical meaning. A man who could induce a multitude to see themselves in him as in a mirror could persuade that multitude that his and their will was, if not higher than the law, then the highest law of the state, and to that law other powers would in point of fact be compelled in the measure of their weakness to comply. Thus Paul's Churchyard challenged a place for itself beside Westminster, and in John Lilburne's demand for free speech the fourth estate demanded constitutional acknowledgment of its legitimate right.

Seen from this point of view, Lilburne cannot be set down as merely a quarrelsome, pig-headed, impractical agitator, "animated by a pharasaic love of self-applause." [113] He did not, true, seek to further the ends that the authorities before which he appeared regarded as justice. His endeavor was always to create a noisy scene which would put himself and his cause before the public eye. He would disrupt the court by some dramatic gesture.of defiance, some refusal to swear an oath, remove his hat, or hold his tongue. If the affair came to the stage of argument, he had always shifts to put his opponents in the wrong. Remanded to prison, he could contrive to put forth a pamphlet in which the mob might have the whole case with all the antecedent particulars, the argument and the law as he saw it, and as they were quite ready to see it too. Prison was but a point of vantage from which to get the public ear. Persecution could be defeated by being made to serve the uses of publicity.

Lilburne's pamphlets on the whole do not make attractive reading. They lack the charm of Walwyn and the coherent strength of Overton at his best. The shorter manifestoes such as the *Letter* to Prynne of January 15, 1645, have a blazing vitality, but the long polemics come tumbling forth, rivers of words. Lilburne wrote in hot haste for an audience which had learned to regard anything he said or did as news. He needed not so much to persuade as to tell the story which they already knew in part, to express what they felt and thought, to get their common grievances aired. He writes like a man talking all night in a tavern to his own partisans. Thus in *Innocency and Truth* (January 6), 1646, he sets out to retry his case against Prynne both in the matter of printing

[113] Morley, *Cromwell*, 280; Masson, *Milton*, III, 388.

without license and of the reparation of his losses. But that leads him into long autobiographical digressions — his appearance before the House of Commons, his conduct at the capture of Tickhill Castle, the treasons of Manchester and the peculations of Colonel King, the oppressions of the Merchant Adventurers. Every now and then, he veers back to Prynne, and finally concludes with citations of the greatest interest from Coke's *Institutes*, Parker's *Observations* and Saint Germain's *Doctor and Student*. But he is always timely, apposite, racily circumstantial concerning things that really mattered to the thousands who found themselves so far only the worse off by the substitution of Parliament for king, of presbyter for prelate.

Less chaotic in structure, *Englands Birth-Right* is a tract which can be perused by the modern reader with more sustained comprehension. It is of special interest in that here Lilburne supplies the mob of distressed tradesmen, artisans and soldiers with a considered statement of principles and grievances. The opening pages, indeed, state the constitutional demands which henceforth for generations would be reiterated by leaders of the populace. Law must be subject to equity, and rulers must be subject to law. The fundamental laws of the state, moreover, must be written down so that men may know their rights. Casting about to find the body of basic law, Lilburne fastens upon Magna Charta as the supreme charter of popular liberty. On this footing, he proceeds to the statement of leading questions, covering the legal rights he clamored for in his own defense against successive persecutions. But he then moves on to put the case for economic justice, significantly linked with liberty of conscience and freedom of the press. Seeing that Parliament has abolished the patents for soap, salt and leather, what justice is there in its present granting of a monopoly of the word of God to the clergy, of wool to the Merchant Adventurers, of printing to the Stationers' Company? The ninth and last query is in effect a demand that only men faithful to the principles already expressed be permitted to serve the state. It leads to the statement of a long series of specific accusations of betrayal of those principles. *Englands Birth-Right* thus provided Lilburne's followers with a kind of platform upon which they could organize concerted action, leading to their final effort to impose upon the constitution a fundamental written instrument in the form of an "Agreement of the People."

XIV

THE GREAT CHARTER OF REASON AND EQUITY

[WILLIAM WALWYN]

Englands Lamentable Slaverie [114]

Englands Birth-Right laid claim to a legal basis in Magna Charta for popular rights. Walwyn was quick to come to Lilburne's personal support, but he was no less quick to single out what, to his less lawyerly and more reflective mind, seemed the weak point in Lilburne's reasoning. Reason and equity were one thing; Magna Charta, he thought, was much less. This he made the theme of his anonymous *Englands Lamentable Slaverie* (October 11). After a characteristic assertion of the duty of coming to the aid of good men suffering injustice, even when as in this case one disagrees with them in religion, he warns Lilburne not to be satisfied with a mess of pottage. Magna Charta is good, he says, so far as it goes, but it is merely that little, less than which could not be granted by the strong hand of the people's conqueror. Real reliance may be placed only in open and universal justice and on the judgment of the honest and plain men of England. For the formation and enforcement of that judgment, the event would show, they had power in their own hands. "One single honest-hearted man alone oftimes by unpleasing importunity" may save an army. In the following year, when Lilburne went once more to Newgate, Walwyn elaborated the point still further in *A Pearle in a Dounghill* (June 30), 1646, a brilliant review of Lilburne's career, showing that his only offense had been to know, discover, and attack abuses. But, Walwyn concludes, "the People are becoming a *Knowing* and *Judicious People, Affliction* hath made them *wise,* now *Oppression* maketh wise men mad."

[114] Vol. III, p. 309.

XV

THE POWER OF LOVE AGAIN

WILLIAM WALWYN

A Whisper in the Eare of Mr. Thomas Edwards,[115]
A Prediction of Mr. Edwards his Conversion.[116]

Lilburne might defy the authorities, and men might rally to his support, but the battle for toleration and free speech, so essential to the activities of revolutionary pamphleteers, was as yet far from won. Edwards' hue and cry after heretics veered from the Independents and sectaries to Lilburne and his party. Walwyn had so far consistently allowed his writings to make their own appeal to reason without the support of their author's name, and though he himself moved freely about among the disaffected, his Fabian adroitness had kept him up to this time free from personal embroilment. But Edwards' *Gangraena*, Part I, named him "a Seeker, a dangerous man, a strong head," repeating a story that at some gathering "one Mr. Wallin fell upon the Presbyterian, asking him how he could prove the Scriptures to be the word of God." *Gangraena* II, supplying more particulars, promised moreover a whole book to be written later against him and his fellows, "following him from place to place, from person to person with whom he hath conversed, and from one thing to another that he hath had his hand in." Walwyn is a "desperate, dangerous man, a Seeker and a Libertine, a man of all Religions, pleading for all; and yet what Religion he is of no man can tell; A man of equivocating Jesuiticall spirit, being full of mentall reservations." He has expressed disloyalty to the king, and called godly ministers "a company of Mountebancks" who had no more authority to preach than did cobblers, weavers and soap boilers. He has even said of the Irish

[115] Vol. III, p. 319.   [116] Vol. III, p. 337.

rebels that they "did no more but what we would have done ourselves, if it had been our case; and said, what had the English to do in their Kingdome? and that they were a better natured people than we, and said, why should not they enjoy the liberty of their Consciences." After that, Edwards probably was not surprised to hear that Walwyn at a tavern "spake of the Trinity in such a strange manner" as to break up the company, and that he defended the right of women to disagree with their husbands — "said, they could give a Reason for it, and that it was their Conscience that led them to it." Such was the man whom Hugh Peters to Edwards's alarm was thought to have put upon his list along with Lilburne as a fit candidate for a seat in Parliament.

Thus assailed, Walwyn came out in the open to defend himself in a series of short tracts in which the pamphlet was for once raised to the level of literary art. Edwards was dealt with effectively but humanely. Among all the enemies of intolerance, Walwyn was almost alone in his tolerance of spirit. In the face of all the naked self-righteous greed of the time, he remained true to his faith in the essential reasonableness and good will of human nature. He was able to keep his integrity without losing charity. "I say all the war I have made, hath been to get victory on the understandings of men." He has made injustice his enemy, "so as to destroy the evil but to preserve the person." He is willing to try reason even upon Edwards, and when that fails, he turns not to abuse but to irony. He picks the man up without hurting him, yet so as to let his squirmings show what becomes of one who surrenders to fear, hatred and intolerance. *A Whisper in the Eare of Mr. Thomas Edwards* (March 13), 1646, written in reply to *Gangraena*, I, is a brief autobiographical account of one who has learned to regard all men as conscientious, to avoid taking upon himself peremptorily to determine truth and error, and to find peace in considering and in drawing others lovingly to consider what is useful for all. The true sectary and schismatic is the man like Edwards of persecuting spirit. *A Word More*

to Mr. Thomas Edwards (March 19) defines schism as "un-
peaceable and violent perversnesse, a disposition impossible
to hold fellowship withall, and hee onely a schismatick that is
such and not an honest quiet spirited person that out of conscience and difference in judgment cannot walk in Church
fellowship with me."

When the second part of *Gangraena* (May 28) appeared,
Walwyn offered *An Antidote Against Master Edwards His
old and New Poyson* (June 10). There he refuses to answer
slanders in detail, but, with humorous penetration and with
the assistance of a keen understanding of Machiavelli, exposes
the motives, methods and desired ends of the self-seeking,
rancorous defender of vested interests. Knowing no doubt
that Edwards had still another blast in preparation, Walwyn
soon returned to the attack with *A Prediction of Mr. Edwards his Conversion, and Recantation* (August 11). So much
persuasion has been bestowed upon the man, surely, Walwyn
thinks, it must by this time be having some effect. Besides, his
very rage against heretics may, as in the case of Paul, indicate
that his conscience secretly condemns him, and be evidence that
he will soon repent. With irony not unworthy of Swift himself, Walwyn then puts into Edwards' mouth a speech of repentance which, without the least break in dramatic propriety,
is perhaps the most brilliant statement that had yet appeared
of the essential points in the doctrine of free conscience. But
he had not yet done with the author of *Gangraena*. Taking
his cue, it may be, from Overton's *Araignement*, he published,
this time anonymously, an allegorical *Parable, or Consulta-
tion of Physitians upon Master Edwards* (October 29). In
this, Doctors Love, Justice, Patience and Truth, summoned
by Conscience, Hope and Piety in opposition to Superstition
and Policie, operate upon Edwards for the removal of a
bladder from his head, source of the gangrene that has been
flowing from his mouth. The sufferer awakes and in the vein
of the recantation of the former tract preaches a sermon on
the text, "The whole commandement is fulfilled in this one
word, Love."

XVI

THE RIGHTS OF MAN

[RICHARD OVERTON]

A Remonstrance of Many Thousand Citizens,
The Commoners Complaint.[117]

William Walwyn was convinced that love and reason were a law of nature which could not be abrogated with impunity, and he saw the folly of Edwards and Prynne pitting their puny spleen against its iron rigor. Lilburne, lawyerlike, must read the law of nature into Magna Charta. The task of turning the statement of the law of nature into a ringing declaration of the rights of man fell to Richard Overton. Against the agitation among the ministers and in the Common Council of the City of London for the enforcement of Presbyterianism, he issued *The Last Warning to all the Inhabitants of London* (March 20), 1646. He admonished his readers that, without the protection of the army, London would be at the mercy of the king, and that without toleration there could be no army. The boldness of this statement so angered the authorities that William Larner, the bookseller who sold the pamphlet, was immediately seized (March 22) by agents of the Stationers' Company and clapped into jail for refusal to answer questions of the Committee for Examinations.[118] When Lilburne was imprisoned in June by the Lords, Overton at once protested in *A Remonstrance of many Thousand Citizens, and other Free-born People of England* (July 7). Still escaping detection, as he had so far done in the Martin tracts, he followed with *An Alarum to the House of Lords* (July 31), which finally led to his arrest (August 11). He

[117] Vol. III, pp. 349, 371.
[118] *A True Relation of . . . the . . . illegal Proceedings against William Larner* (May 2); Joseph Hunscot, *Petition and Information* (June 11).

refused like Lilburne and Larner to acknowledge the Lords' jurisdiction, and so followed the others to Newgate. Thence he sent forth, following their example, a provocative account of his arrest and arraignment, called *A Defiance against all Arbitrary Usurpations or Encroachments, either of the House of Lords, or any other, upon the Soveraignty of the Supreme House of Commons . . . or upon the Rights, Properties and Freedoms of the people in generall* (September 9). He pursued his case further in *An Arrow against all Tyrants and Tyrany, shot from the Prison of New-gate into the Prerogative Bowels of the Arbitrary House of Lords* (October 12). The Lords, in their furious effort to stop the flow of his pen, arraigned him again and sent his wife to Bridewell, not however without provoking from him another exposure of their proceedings in *The Commoners Complaint* (February 10), 1647.

Overton is perhaps our best witness to the force of Lilburne's example, and to the rapid crystallization into dogma of the democratic views which Walwyn had for years been gently pushing. *A Remonstrance* bore as frontispiece the portrait of Lilburne which had first appeared in the latter's *Christian Mans Triall*.[119] It was now printed with iron bars engraved across the face. Like Lilburne, but with more finished eloquence, Overton declares to his persecutors, "I am resolved by the grace of God, that whatsoever either you, or any man, or men shall do against me, I will not let go (by my own or proper consent) the least punctillio, jot, title or harebreadth of the just Rights, freedoms, or liberties either of myself, or of any other individuall, or of this Nation in generall: stand or fall, live or die, come what come will, on this I am resolved, hoping so to deport myself according to the Rule of Reason, equity and justice, that if I suffer, it shall not be for evill, but for well-doing, and righteousnesse sake." [120] In this spirit, as he tells us in *The Commoners Complaint*, his very legs, and his wife's after him, refused to obey. Neither

[119] See above, p. 13.   [120] *Defiance*, 13.

man nor wife would so much as walk to jail; they required the
agents of the House of Lords to drag them through the streets
by main force. But Overton surpasses even Lilburne in the
extremes of assertion as well as of gesture. It is, in terms,
"we the people" for whom he speaks. The people's native
right, upon which the social contract rests, is to name and
instruct rulers to do that which, if it had been convenient,
the people might have done themselves. This right cannot be
destroyed, though the Norman kings and their creatures,
the nobles, not to mention parliaments, churchmen, lawyers
and other slavish instruments of oppression, have done their
utmost to deprive the people of their rights by the formalities
of law and religion, by false sentiment and pageantry, by com-
mercial monopolies and censorship of the press. They have
left to the common man only that beggarly remnant of his
natural rights contained in Magna Charta. But, Overton
asserts, "I'le not sell my birth-right for a messe of pottage,
for Justice is my naturall right, my heirdome, my inheritance
by lineall descent from the loins of *Adam*, and so to all the
sons of men as their proper right without respect of persons." [121] "For by naturall birth, all men are equally and alike
borne to like propriety, liberty and freedome, and as we are
delivered of God by the hand of nature into this world, every-
one with a naturall, innate freedome and propriety (as it
were writ in the table of every mans heart, never to be obli-
terated) even so are we to live, every one equally and alike to
enjoy his Birthright and priviledge; even all whereof God
by nature hath made him free. . . . Every man by nature
being a King, Priest and Prophet in his owne naturall circuite
and compasse, whereof no second may partake, but by deputation, commission, and free consent from him, whose right
and freedome it is." [122]

Such sentiments were, of course, not wholly new, nor were
they peculiar to Overton and his associates. Upon some such
grounds, in fact, were Milton in his *Tenure of Kings and*

[121] *Ibid.*, 6.   [122] *Arrow*, 3-4.

Magistrates (February 13), 1649, and Goodwin in his *Right and Might well met* (January 2), to defend the execution of Charles. What was notable in Overton's tracts was the vigor and clarity with which, in accents that hark forward to Tom Paine and the Declaration of Independence, they marshall the dogmas of natural liberty in support of popular government, of toleration and freedom of the press, of the abolition of tithes, monopolies and imprisonment for debt.

XVII

THE CALL FOR AN AGREEMENT OF THE PEOPLE

To the right Honourable and supreme Authority of this Nation, the Commons in Parliament Assembled.[123]

Liberty was not to be secured, in 1646, merely by pamphlets, however bold and clear, nor even by going to jail for publishing them without license. Lilburne and Overton, though it seemed impossible by any means totally to silence them, were behind bars. Yet if their cause were to be advanced, popular pressure had to be brought by other persons to bear effectively upon the House of Commons. If that failed, recourse must be had to the army, where, it became increasingly plain, the real power in the state lay.

Who was the chief actor in the organization of the Leveller party in the developments of 1647 and after, one could not in the present state of the evidence venture to assert. Walwyn's share in that work was, however, considerable. His previous activities show him to have been a man who sought influence over others rather than personal acclaim. He was in the habit of coming to the assistance of other men against persecution. He had grown adept from long practice in seeking to win victories over men's understandings. He thought that his belief in the efficacy of love and reason might come to practical fruition in a state composed of local democracies united by a popular representative body and limited by fundamental law to the peaceful maintenance of free play for faith, discussion and enterprise. That in the movement for popular sympathy evoked by Lilburne and Overton, Walwyn saw his opportunity to play compassionate Samaritan on a larger scale and with more far-reaching effect than he had yet attained is at least a plausible inference.

[123] Vol. III, p. 397.

The Levellers took form as a party during the early months of 1647, in the support of a series of petitions to the House of Commons demanding the enactment of revolutionary constitutional changes to accord with the principles and reforms which Lilburne, Walwyn and Overton had been advocating, and which appear again in the Leveller *Agreement of the People* published in 1648. Of this series, the most important was a "large" petition, a copy of which was intercepted and prematurely brought to the House (March 15). A second, supporting petition was presented a little later, only to be condemned. When the "large" petition was at length formally submitted, it was condemned to be burnt by the common hangman (May 20). A third petition was also rejected a few days later, and shortly after that appeared a brief pamphlet, *Gold tried in the fire* (June 14), defending all three petitions and reciting the circumstances of their condemnation. The "large" petition itself seems not to have been published until the ensuing year.[124]

Petition and pamphlet were undoubtedly the work of Walwyn. No other writer among the Levellers could have put the case so clearly, so incisively, or with so much dignity and intelligence. At a later time, moreover, Walwyn said that his ideas on government would be found in "that large petition that was burnt by the common Hangman."[125] The evidence thus provided of the part he had played in organizing popular support for the Leveller movement is curiously supplemented by the testimony of men who had, for a time at least, aided him. In their opposition to persecution, the Levellers had found allies in the Independent and Separatist ministers, and Walwyn himself had defended Goodwin and been assisted by his congregation.[126] Walwyn's rational and inquiring temper, his scepticism in theology, and his anticlericalism were, however, not traits of which men like Goodwin and the other ministers could approve. When they turned upon the Levellers, therefore, in support of the Council of State in

---

[124] *To the right Honourable and supreme Authority* (September 19), 1648.
[125] *Fountain of Slaunder*, 7.   [126] See above, p. 101.

1649, Walwyn was the man singled out as the one really dangerous member of the party. The manifesto called *Walwins Wiles* (May 10), 1649, and dedicated to Parliament by William Kiffen, John Price and five other men, was probably the work of Price, a supporter of John Goodwin.[127] Whoever among them held the pen, certainly they had all had abundant opportunity to watch the Levellers at their work, and their description of the characters of the radical leaders, prejudiced though it be, corresponds shrewdly to what we can learn from friendlier sources. Lilburne they characterize as a saintly well-meaning man, too much given to pride. Overton they know little about. Walwyn is the chief object of their attack. He it is who has corrupted young men by ingratiating manners and artful discourse, teaching them as of their own motion to question the devices and motives of magistrates and of ministers. He has chosen men of wit, cool temper and good language to be his intimates. He has set the fiery-tempered ones to writing pamphlets. He has seen to it that the "miscarriages" of government should "be printed and published to the world, and these books must be dispersed especially among the known wel-affected and forward party in all places, to which end it must be so ordered and managed, that these books may be upon free cost scattered abroad in the Countries, and all those places and Counties especially that are adjacent to the City of *London*." [128] Finally came peremptory petitions intended to subvert the government, which Walwyn arranged to have signed by large numbers of deluded persons and presented to Parliament. Such was the picture which Walwyn's enemies drew of him, but hostile in the extreme as it was, he denied in his replies not the activities attributed to him so much as the interpretation placed upon them.

The burning of the "large" petition marked the end of the Levellers' effort to effect the modern democratic state by act of the Long Parliament. The Presbyterian party had in the meantime reached a deadlock in their dealings with the New

[127] Brooke, *The Charity of Churchmen.*
[128] *Walwins Wiles*, 16

Model. In a few days, Cornet Joyce was to take Charles into his custody. The Levellers turned like other men to the army, in whose hands political power now lay, and their ideas were next to find expression in the debates of the Army Council, in the several attempts to arrive at an Agreement of the People, and in a new crop of pamphlets. They were finally to be stilled for the time by the hand of Cromwell.

It was true, as Gardiner says, that the "large" petition was a program not for a single Parliament but for three hundred years. Yet, when no party in the state was able to plan effectively for the moment, it was no discredit to Walwyn and his associates that they laid down so clearly the path which three centuries in England and America were step by step to pursue. The "large" petition was the natural outcome of the series of events and discussions initiated when Lilburne was scattering unlicensed pamphlets from the pillory to the mob, and when Walwyn was trying in the spirit of Montaigne to learn what was really useful in the dreams of the Familists. It put into practical and rational terms the discontents and mystical strivings of a class which had still much to learn concerning its own powers as well as its own rights in society. Burned in 1647, that petition nevertheless contained ideas which were destined to become the revolutionary commonplaces of the future.

APPENDICES

APPENDIX A

THE WRITINGS OF WILLIAM WALWYN

The primary source of information concerning the writings of William Walwyn is to be found in his acknowledged tracts. Except in two instances, these were written in self-defence. They supply vivid biographical details which reveal a personality of striking and unusual quality. These tracts are: *A Whisper in the Eare of Mr. Thomas Edwards* (March 13), 1646; *A Word More to Mr. Thomas Edwards* (March 13); *An Antidote against Master Edwards* (June 10); *A Prediction of Mr. Edwards his Conversion* (August 11); *A Still Small Voice*, 1647 (McAlpin Collection; not in the British Museum); *The Fountain of Slaunder* (May 30); *Walwyn's Just Defence*, 1649 (McAlpin Collection and, according to Pease, the Newberry Library, Chicago; not in the British Museum); and *Juries Justified* (December 2), 1651. *A Manifestation* (April 14), 1649, and *An Agreement of the Free People of England* (May 1), were both published in collaboration with Lilburne, Prince and Overton. Additional information will be found in *The Charity of Churchmen* (May 28), 1649, a defense of Walwyn by his friend Henry Brooke; in Lilburne's *Letter to a Friend* and *Innocency and Truth*, and in Bastwick's *Just Defence* (Walwyn's name appearing in each of these three works as "Worley" or "Worly"); in Edwards' *Gangraena*, I, II, III; in *Walwins Wiles*, by William Kiffen and others; and in Lilburne's *Picture of the Council of State*.

In addition to the tracts mentioned above, certain others are directly or indirectly acknowledged by Walwyn himself or by his friend Brooke in his behalf. These are: *A Helpe to the Right Understanding* (February 6), 1646; *A Word in Season* (May 18); and *A Parable* (October 29). Certain allusions in *Fountain of Slaunder* and *Walwyns Just Defence* also point clearly to his authorship of the Levellers' "large" petition of May 20, 1647, together with the prefatory statement, *Gold Tried in the Fire* (June 14), 1647, with which it was intended to be published, and of *The Vanitie of the Present Churches* (March 12), 1649.

Certain facts concerning the printing of the above-mentioned tracts of 1646 seem to confirm the attributions which I have made, though in view of the state of printing at the time, all such evidence must be used with abundant reservation. Thomas Paine, who took up his freedom in 1628, had a shop in Goldsmith's Alley, Redcrosse Street, Cripplegate, from 1630 to 1650(?). The four pamphlets which Walwyn issued in 1646 over his own name (*Whisper, Word More, Antidote, Prediction*), all bore Paine's imprint. Two pamphlets acknowledged later (*Word in Season, Parable*), and one here attributed to Walwyn on internal evidence, were also printed by Paine. The remaining pamphlets of 1646 here attributed to Walwyn (*The Just Man, Pearle, Demurre*) are closely similar in typography to Paine's known work. One (*The Afflicted Christian*), which merely includes a letter which I attribute to Walwyn, resembles the work of the secret press of Overton and Larner.[1] I have found in the Thomason Collection only four other publications of 1646 with Paine's imprint. Walwyn's later tracts seem to have been done by other printers. The evidence, inconclusive as it is, seems to suggest that during this year, at least, Walwyn employed Paine, and that the latter put forth little other acknowledged work.

The idiosyncracies of personality, style and point of view, manifested in the works mentioned above, are singularly characteristic and sustained. None of these tracts could have been written by any other pamphleteer of the time known to me. Walwyn writes with a peculiar lucidity, ease, candor and de-

[1] See above, p. 90.

tached irony touched with imagination. He reiterates in picked phrases his belief in love and reason, his anticlericalism, his practice of inquiring into the beliefs of men whose religious convictions he does not share, and of coming to the aid of those who are persecuted for their opinions, and he maintains at all times a tone which can best be described as reminiscent of Montaigne, whom he had read in Florio's translation with approval and admiration.[2] On the basis of this unique combination of qualities, I have little hesitation in concluding that Walwyn was the author of *Some Considerations* (November 10), 1642; *The Power of Love* (September 19), 1643; and *The Compassionate Samaritane*, 1644, including, as it did originally, *Good Counsell* (July 29), 1644. These little tracts, as special pleas on behalf of the sects by one who professes to be no sectary himself, are plainly all by the same hand, but no hand but Walwyn's would have opened what purports to be a Familist sermon on *The Power of Love* with an evident free rendering from Montaigne's essay on cannibals of a passage on the state of nature. Some confirmation of these attributions also comes from statements of Henry Brooke and, I think, from my own experience in dealing with the bibliographical problem presented by *The Compassionate Samaritane*.

Brooke says, "And for Liberty of Conscience, there is a book (the first that was brought to light upon that Subject, since these Troubles) doth ow much to his Industry: And though he is not so much concern'd in the point as other men, especially his Adversaries (he having never bin of any private Congregation) yet did he one of the first break the Ice in that point, since this Parliament, and to the utmost of his power, both by writing and by frequent and very hazardable Addresses to Authority, labored both to evince the equity of the thing it itself, and procure a Liberty for the Exercise thereof."[3] These words suit more exactly the four pamphlets just mentioned than any others of the same period which I have

[2] *Just Defence.*   [3] *Charity of Churchmen,* 11.

seen dealing with the same subject. They have sometimes
been taken to refer to *Liberty of Conscience* (March 24),
1644, attributed by Firth to Henry Robinson.[4] That the two
men had at one time some acquaintance with one another
is evidenced by Walwyn's *Juries Justified*, and the attitude
toward persecution in *Liberty of Conscience* may show his
influence. Like Robinson's other tracts, however, the work is
informed with the results of the latter's observations in foreign
lands, whereas Walwyn never traveled abroad and affected
to scorn Robinson for having done so.[5]

The Compassionate Samaritane appears in the Thomason
Collection as "The Second *Edition*, corrected and enlarged
1644[5]." Thomason entered the date "January 5" and
"much" before "enlarged." On July 29, he had already entered in his collection a thin little pamphlet in precisely the
same format, called *Good Counsell to all*, though without
separate title-page, and with pages numbered 79-92. He
wrote across the top, "This is all of this booke though it begins
thus." Upon internal evidence I surmised that this too was
by Walwyn, and had originally been intended as part of *The
Compassionate Samaritane*. My impression was confirmed upon my discovery in the library of Yale University of a copy
of the first edition of *The Compassionate Samaritane*. It there
appeared that the work, a tiny pamphlet, originally consisted
of two parts in addition to the epistle or preface. The first
(pages 7-71) was headed *Liberty of Conscience Asserted
and the Separatist Vindicated*, the second (pages 72-83) *Good
Counsell to all*. This edition must have been published soon
after Thomas Bakewell's *Confutation of the Anabaptists*, to
which it refers and which was entered by Thomason in his
collection on June 21, 1644. The second edition, to which
Thomason assigns the date, January 5, 1645, includes only
the prefatory epistle and *Liberty of Conscience Asserted*,
completely omitting *Good Counsell to all*. It is much enlarged,
chiefly in being printed with wider spaces on somewhat larger

---

[4] See above, p. 67, n. 56.   [5] *Juries Justified*.

paper, the pages being numbered 1-79. *Good Counsell to all*, to which Thomason assigns the date, July 29, 1644, reappears as a separate fragment in precisely the same format, the pages being numbered 79-92. I surmise that the facts may be explained somewhat as follows. In the first place, we must remember that Thomason did not always succeed in securing copies of pamphlets for his collection directly upon publication. Bakewell's *Confutation* may have appeared somewhat earlier than June 21. Walwyn probably published the first edition of *The Compassionate Samaritane* early in July or late in June, but the work escaped Thomason. Walwyn prepared a second edition for the press almost immediately after the appearance of the first. He originally intended to include *Good Counsell to all* as before, and this was already in type as pages 79-92, when he decided to remove it. He then expanded the concluding paragraphs of *Liberty of Conscience Asserted* sufficiently to fill up a new page 79, and issued the latter work as "The Second *Edition*, corrected, and enlarged" of *The Compassionate Samaritane*. At the same time, he issued the discarded pages of *Good Counsell to all* as a separate publication. Thomason, though he may have seen the first and complete edition, did not connect the two parts of the second. He secured a copy of *Good Counsell to all* on July 29, but the main work, which must have appeared at about the same time, eluded him until the following January. I have not seen a copy of the first edition which is reported to be in the Bodleian. Masson, without stating his evidence, says that *The Compassionate Samaritane* appeared "about the middle of 1644," but dismisses it with the remark that "it need be remembered by its name only." [6]

Certain other pamphlets may be attributed to Walwyn from internal evidence and the probability suggested by attendant circumstances. The earliest of these is *Englands Lamentable Slaverie* (October 11), 1645, attributed to Walwyn "at a guess" by Pease.[7] He was probably the author of a letter

[6] *Milton*, III, 112.   [7] *Leveller Movement*, 116; see above, pp. 37-38.

to Thomas Hawes, published in *The Afflicted Christian* (May 18), 1646, and had a hand in *Vox Populi, or the Peoples Cry against the Clergy* (August 26).[8] His effort on Lilburne's behalf in 1646 is doubtless to be seen in the two very similar tracts of identical date, *The Just Man in Bonds* (June 29) and *A Pearle in a dounghill* (June 30),[9] and his protest against the proposed ordinance against heresy in *A Demurre to the Bill* (October 7).[10] It is, finally, natural to conclude that he played an important part in drafting the Levellers' first *Agreement of the People* (1647),[11] as well as that which appeared later over his name as collaborator.[12]

Pease, largely on the suggestion of Brooke's remarks quoted above, ventures the surmise that Walwyn wrote *The Humble Petition of the Brownists* (November), 1641.[13] Pease does not note that this was practically identical with *A New Petition of the Papists* (September), 1641. Who the author was, it is impossible to say, but I suspect some Catholic hand, and feel that the attribution to Walwyn is doubtful. These tracts, though vigorously written, differ markedly from Walwyn's in style, and are lacking in Walwyn's recurrent insistence upon love and reason as the way to social unity. Brooke's statement is better explained as I have indicated above. *The Bloody Project* (August 21), 1648, published as by "W. P., Gent.," was attributed to Walwyn in an anonymous reply, *The Discoverer* (June 2), 1649. This attribution, though not denied by Henry Brooke in his rejoinder, *The Craft-mens Craft* (June 25), seems in the light of internal evidence dubious. Walwyn was arrested by the Council of State upon the charge of having a share in *Englands New Chaines Discovered* (February 26), 1649, but the authorship of that work was acknowledged by Lilburne, Overton and Prince in the second edition (March 24) with no mention of Walwyn.

In concluding this note, I wish to state that no one realizes better than I the chances for error in any attempt to determine

8 See above, p. 92, n. 93.   9 See above, p. 107.
10 See above, p. 85.   11 Gardiner, *Constitutional Documents*, 333.
12 See above, p. 116.   13 *Leveller Movement*, 256-257.

the authorship of pamphlets of this period. The attributions here suggested have been made only after a reading in chronological order of most of the Thomason Collection for the years concerned, and by noting the highly individual common characteristics of the pamphlets in question. Not a few plausible guesses at Walwyn's authorship in other cases have been dismissed. At the same time, I am not confident of having discovered everything he may have written or had part in.

MILTON'S REPUTATION AND INFLUENCE, 1643-1647

The known circumstances of Milton's life during the years of his marriage and separation from his wife, the years in which he produced his tracts on divorce and his *Areopagitica*, are few and puzzling. One would naturally expect, judging from the habits of controversy at the time, that the private affairs, particularly the marital difficulties, of the author of *The Doctrine and Discipline of Divorce* could hardly fail to have attracted attention in the pamphlets of the period. One would expect, too, that an argument for toleration and freedom of the press, coming from the author of so notorious a book as that on divorce, would have evoked particularly hostile notice. These expectations are not fulfilled. A few years ago, the present writer made a brief excursion into the pamphlet literature immediately preceding *Areopagitica* with the purpose of verifying Masson's findings in respect to the place of that work in the discussions of 1644.[1] Led by the discovery that Masson's acquaintance with the pamphlets was limited and erratic, the writer undertook a systematic search through the contemporary literature of the decade from 1640 to 1650 in the hope of turning up allusions to the poet that Masson may have missed. He will not be so rash as to say that nothing escaped him, but little has been found. Though the impression that Masson's knowledge was incomplete has been confirmed, it must be admitted that he managed with one important exception to catch all the significant references to his hero. His interpretation of those references, on the other hand, suffers egregiously from the Carlylean attitude of mind by which he was obsessed, and from his failure to do

---

[1] *Before Areopagitica*, PMLA, XLII, 1927.

justice to what he regarded as the lower and less pleasant aspects of Milton's contemporary background. The inferences to be drawn in the light of the time from the paucity of allusions to Milton in the pamphlets and from the character of those few that do occur run plainly counter to the impression conveyed by Masson in the third volume of his *Life*. The truth seems to be that Milton was personally little known to the general public, and was not regarded as a person of importance until after he became identified with the revolutionary leaders of 1649. He did not align himself with Independents like John Goodwin, or with champions of the sects and leaders of the populace like Lilburne and Richard Overton. Roger Williams he knew, but doubtless only through common acquaintance with Sir Henry Vane, himself personally removed from popular levels of revolutionary activity.

The ignorance concerning Milton's personal character and affairs, shown during these years by his opponents, is curiously complete. Bishop Hall and his son,[2] who must surely have had means of finding out whatever there was to their purpose to be found out concerning their antagonist in 1642, seem to have relied upon rumor, invention and dubious inferences based upon the raciness of Milton's vocabulary. Except for the replies of the Halls, Milton's antiprelatical tracts went unnoticed in the press. *The Doctrine and Discipline of Divorce* [first edition (August 1), 1643; second edition (February 2), 1644] soon achieved notoriety as a scandalous book. It was commonly linked with Roger Williams' *The Bloudy Tenent* (July 15), 1644, and Richard Overton's *Mans Mortallitie* (January 19), 1644. This association was due merely to the facts that the three works appeared during the controversy raised by the *Apologeticall Narration* at the opening

---

[2] *Modest Confutation* (January), 1642. B. A. Wright (*Modern Language Review*, XXVI, XXVII) argues convincingly that Milton's first marriage must have occurred in 1642, not, as has traditionally been supposed, in 1643. *Modest Confutation* appeared in January before the marriage. The occurence of Milton's marital misadventure at the earlier date in the circumstances of haste and privacy described by Wright may account for the ignorance of the matter shown by his opponents in and after 1644.

of 1644, and that each presented what was commonly regarded as a most shocking heresy — divorce; the toleration
of Jews, Papists, Turks, and pagans; the mortality of the soul.
These were notions which the faithful could and no doubt
generally did condemn on hearsay without having to read the
books in which they were advanced. The anonymous reply
to *The Doctrine and Discipline of Divorce* [*Answer* (November 19), 1644] does show acquaintance with Milton's book,
but none with Milton himself, a striking lack, since the author
would surely have had no scruples of delicacy in making use
of knowledge of Milton's marital unhappiness, if he had
happened to possess any. Other references to the divorce
tract, and they are limited solely to the first of the series that
Milton put forth, are conspicuously uniform in brevity and
vagueness. In most cases, there is nothing to indicate that
the persons who damned the heresy had been at pains to read
the book. Milton is sometimes mentioned, sometimes not. He
is, at best, only a name. None of the men who attacked his
ideas on marriage seem to have known that his wife had left
him, and none gave serious consideration to the ideas. Divorce
merely takes its place among the more revolting errors which
were supposed to be resulting from delay in reformation
of church government on Presbyterian lines. Thus Herbert
Palmer, in his sermon [3] preached August 13, 1644, while
naming over opinions that ought to be suppressed, recommends
that the book on divorce be burnt. The Commons order of
August 24, prompted by a petition from the Stationers' Company, merely gave direction in general terms that persons
responsible for the publication of "pamphlets against the Immortality of the Soul and concerning Divorce" be apprehended
and punished.[4] In the Stationers' response to the Lords in
December, 1644, Milton's name was mentioned along with
that of Hezekiah Woodward as the author of a scandalous
book.[5] Complaints from the Westminster Assembly included
Milton, but only together with Roger Williams, Clement

[3] *Glasse of Gods Providence.*   [4] Masson, *Milton*, III, 164-165.
[5] Masson, III, 293.

Wrighter — supposed author of *Mans Mortallitie* — John Goodwin, and others.[6]

All this indicates that Milton's advocacy of divorce was shocking to contemporaries, not at all that his book was widely read or that he himself was well known or influential. Frenzied controversialists, seeking to foment popular apprehension, seized upon divorce as one among several examples of the devastating errors that would be sure to run rife if toleration were allowed. The same impression is created by the allusions that followed with some frequency in the pamphlets of the Presbyterians. Prynne alludes in passing to "divorce at pleasure" and "soules mortality." [7] Featley cites "a Tractate on Divorce, in which the bonds of marriage are let loose to inordinate lust," [8] and in the same sentence damns *The Bloudy Tenent* and *Mans Mortallitie*. Pagitt in *Heresiography* (May 8), 1645, repeats almost verbatim what Featley had said concerning the three pamphlets, and contributes on the title-page a picture of "a Divorcer," attended by other pictures representing an Anabaptist, a Familist, a Jesuit, an Antinomian and a Seeker. *Heresiography* was typical of a class of publications of which there were numerous examples. The manner was to present with appropriate expressions of horror a catalogue of the heresies of the day. One such publication merely rang the changes on its predecessors, and divorce naturally passed with little variation from one to another. Thus *A Catalogue of the severall Sects and Opinions in England* (January 19), 1647, which appeared as a broadside with rude cuts, pictured "Divorcer" as Pagitt had done, accompanied by "Soule Sleeper" and other heretics, each picture being attended by suitable verses of disapproval. Another broadside, called *These Tradesmen are Preachers* (April 26), 1647, listed divorce among the forty-nine errors which it attributed to tradesmen and mechanics, who were represented by crude engravings portraying a confectioner, a tailor and the like.

[6] Masson, III, 165.
[7] *Twelve Considerable Serious Questions* (September 16) 1644.
[8] *Dippers Dipt* (February 7), 1645.

Similar but more elaborate catalogues were often included in works of larger scope and greater pretension. Particularly noteworthy, as revealing how little Milton was known to controversial divines and pamphleteers, is the reference in *A Dissuasive from the Errours of the Time* (January 22), 1646, by Robert Baillie, one of the Scotch commissioners to the Westminster Assembly, a particularly active and well-known figure. Enumerating the tenets of the Independents, Baillie mentions "a large treatise" in which "Mr. Milton" "hath pleaded for a full liberty for any man to put away his wife, whenever he pleaseth," a statement which may be no more than an echo of Prynne's "divorce at pleasure." Now Masson says "I believe, in fact, that, could Milton's acquaintanceships in London from the winter of 1643-4 onwards be traced and recovered, they would be found to have been chiefly among the Independents, Anabaptists, Antinomians, Seekers and other Tolerationists." Baillie, on the other hand, follows the reference to Milton which has just been cited, by the candid admission that "I doe not know certainely whether this man professeth Independency." All he knows is that Milton is the author of the heresy concerning divorce, and "all the Hereticks here, whereof ever I heard, avow themselves Independents." Aware, however, that he cannot of his own knowledge identify Milton as an Independent, and yet at the same time desirous of fastening the advocacy of divorce upon the Independents, Baillie is forced to conclude by saying in effect that at any rate Independents in New England were well known to have favored divorce; "whatever therefore may be said of Mr. Milton [*i.e.*, as to Independency] yet Mr. Gorting and his company were men of renown among the New-England Independents . . . and all of them doe maintaine, that it is lawfull for every woman to desert her husband, when he is not willing to follow her in a Church way." The vagueness of this statement, as it concerns Milton, is significant. The outstanding "tolerationist" and chief recognized enemy of the Presbyterians among the London Independents was by

1646 John Goodwin. If Milton's acquaintances after 1643 were, as Masson thought, to be found chiefly in "tolerationist" circles, he would surely by 1646 have been in some sort of association with John Goodwin. In that case, Baillie would just as certainly have known of that fact, and would not have hesitated, as he did, to assert it. Neither would he, one hardly needs to add, have hesitated to identify Milton with any of the other groups mentioned by Masson, if he had had information to warrant him in so doing. The truth appears to be that Baillie felt himself to be on surer ground as to Samuel Gorton than as to Milton, and that he knew of Milton only as the author of the divorce tract. The vagueness of his information concerning Milton points to the conclusion that the latter continued after 1643 to hold aloof from all organized partisan groups.

This impression is strongly enforced when we turn to Edwards' *Gangraena*. *Part I* of this work (February 26), 1646, lists 180 heresies, and names many heretical books, some of them several times. Divorce finds its place, though not a prominent one, in this catalogue. A marginal note advises the reader to see "Miltons doctrine of divorce," and it would appear that Edwards had himself read the book. *Part I* also begins the account of Mrs. Attaway, lacewoman and she-preacher, who was reputed to have run away from her husband in company with the husband of another woman. *Gangraena*, *Part II* (May 28), 1646, which devotes some space to tales of immorality and marital irregularity among the sectaries, reports that Mrs. Attaway was heard to commend "Master Miltons Doctrine of Divorce." *Gangraena, Part III*, (December 28), 1646, makes no mention of Milton but accuses the sectaries of claiming that incest and divorce are not sinful. Edwards, it must be remembered, was the self-appointed scavenger of gossip relating to the Independents, sectaries, and advocates of toleration. His avowed purpose was to supply not arguments but facts. His three volumes are stuffed with circumstantial personal detail. Every whisper that came to him which could be interpreted as discreditable to any antagonist of the Presbyterians or their aims seems to have gone into his pages. He tells us that John Goodwin played at bowls on a fast day, that Lilburne played cards, and that Walwyn asked embarassing questions one night at an inn, but he tells us nothing about Milton except that he wrote the divorce tract. If, as Masson surmises (III, 187), there had been gossip concerning Milton in the booksellers' shops near St. Paul's, Edwards would certainly have heard of it, and if he had heard of it, he would have printed it with alacrity. As it is, he can tell us a circumstantial story concerning Mrs. Attaway, but to our great disappointment nothing at all concerning Mrs. Milton. Again the conclusion is inescapable. Milton's affairs were not known to Edwards, for the reason that Milton was not known in the circles of the Independents, sectaries and Levellers, among whom Edwards in his own fashion knew at least something about everybody of any importance whatever, knew something about even the elusive Walwyn, that student of persecution who took pains not to be persecuted.[9]

Areopagitica (November 24), 1644, seems to have contributed nothing to Milton's contemporary reputation and influence. As has been shown, the controversy occasioned by the *Apologetical Narration* emboldened all dissenting minorities and united them in a common demand for toleration. All contention between the Presbyterians and their divers opponents from the opening of 1644 to the second civil war in 1647 converged upon the central issue of toleration and liberty of conscience. The champions of Presbyterianism were compelled to reply in pamphlet after pamphlet to the published arguments and organized efforts of their opponents on this point. The most notable of these replies prior to *Areopagitica* have already been discussed in these pages.[10] Representative

[9] If the facts are as here represented, Saurat's suggestion (*Milton, Man and Thinker*, 310-322) that Milton made one of a so-called sect of "mortalists" responsible for the publication of *Mans Mortallitie* in 1644, so far as it is based on Masson's account of Milton at this time, is untenable.

[10] See above, pp. 51-52.

of Presbyterian polemic after the appearance of Milton's tract in November were Gillespie's *Wholesome Severitie* (January 8), 1645; Vicars' *Picture of Independency* (March 15), 1645, and *Schismatick Sifted* (June 22, 1646); Prynne's *Fresh Discovery* (July 24); and the works of Baillie and Edwards which have just been mentioned. In the pages of these and many similar pamphlets, the publications supporting toleration were singled out for dissection and castigation, and their authors held up for rebuke. They show that the men regarded as most dangerous by those to whom Milton was opposed were first of all John Goodwin and his followers, and then as excitement grew more intense, Lilburne, Walwyn and Overton. The pamphlets most frequently condemned for their advocacy of toleration, though few escaped some mention, were *The Compassionate Samaritane* (probably by Walwyn), *The Bloudy Tenent* by Roger Williams, *Theomachia* and subsequent works by John Goodwin, and the various tracts put forth by Lilburne and Overton. *Areopagitica*, notwithstanding its author's divorce heresy, seems to have gone completely unnoticed. It appears incredible that Milton's great plea for freedom of the press should have failed of any mention whatever in the thousands of pages printed at the time and abounding in specific references to hundreds of other publications, but the present writer is constrained to report that after a protracted search he has failed to find a single one. Surely, if the appearance of *Areopagitica* were ever to be noted, it should have been by Prynne in that chapter of his *Fresh Discovery*, written according to Thomason's dating about six months after the publication of *Areopagitica*, and devoted to the recent attacks upon the printing ordinance. But Prynne assails Henry Robinson, Lilburne, and the anonymous tracts of Overton, completely ignoring Milton.

In the light of these facts, we must dismiss the notion that *Areopagitica* had any appreciable effect on the situation in 1644.[11] Masson surmises that Lilburne had imbibed Milton's

---

[11] Masson, *Milton*, III, 431-434.

lesson and very phraseology, but we have seen Lilburne defending free speech on the pillory as early as 1637, and he might have learned what else he needed to know about liberty from many publications prior to *Areopagitica*. Masson also thinks that the mock order from the Westminster Assembly, prefixed to *The Araignment of Mr. Persecution*, was suggested by the specimen imprimaturs jocularly cited by Milton. But Overton was modeling his mockery on the Marprelate tracts. Masson's most serious misapprehension is, however, of the effect of *Areopagitica* upon the enforcement of the printing ordinance. He would have us believe that by Milton's persuasion the licensers grew more lax. The fact is that from the adoption of the printing ordinance in 1643, directed against royalists and prelatists, the licensers differed among themselves in their attitude toward the issues that rose between the Presbyterians and their various opponents. As the controversy developed, some naturally leaned further to the one side some to the other, and the pamphleteers meanwhile grew bolder and more numerous. The whole system of censorship in fact tended to break down. In support of his view of Milton's part in all this, Masson cites the complaint made by Edwards [12] that John Bachiler, one of the twelve licensers appointed in 1643 to approve books in divinity, acted as "Licenser general of Books, not only of Independent Doctrines, but of Books for a Toleration of all Sects." This, according to Masson, shows that Bachiler had been won over by *Areopagitica*. The fact is that Bachiler's liberalism was in evidence before the publication of Milton's tract, and was probably derived in part from Anabaptist sources, possibly from Walwyn's early anonymous apologies for the sects, and certainly in some measure from John Goodwin. Bachiler approved the publication of Walwyn's *Prediction,* and the republication (April 25), 1646, of the Anabaptist Leonard Busher's plea for toleration, *Religious Peace*, first published in 1614. He also gave his imprimatur to pamphlets by John

[12] *Gangraena*, I, II.

Saltmarsh, a forerunner of the Quakers. More immediately to the point, however, is the fact that he approved Goodwin's *Theomachia* a month or more, accepting Thomason's dating, before *Areopagitica* came out. More significant still is the statement appended by Bachiler to Goodwin's *Twelve Considerable Cautions* (February 17), 1646, in which he attempted to defend himself against Edwards. This statement, which apparently Masson did not see, is interesting not only for its reference to Milton but also for the evidence it gives of the wide diffusion of ideas which it has been too much the custom to attribute in some exclusive fashion to Milton's initiation. Bachiler writes as follows:

Impartial Reader;

Although these ensuing *Cautions about Reformation*, may seeme to give occasion of distaste to such spirits as are wont to be presently tossed in a tempest of prejudice, and their own unquiet passions, before they have read and considered, or have given any leisure to their own reason to debate matters within themselves, yet for mine own part, after the perusal of them, I find nothing expressed therein, contrary to sound doctrine or good manners, therefore allow them to be printed: Ingenuously professing, that as I have been, and still shall be very carefull, that nothing may be authorized under my hand, which shall rationally appeare to me, to be prejudiciall to the Propagation of the Gospel, the Authority of Parliament, or the publique peace; for in this discussing and Truth-searching age, I hold it my duty (whatever the censures of some may be) even as a man, much more as a Christian, (in all sober and calm disputes from Scripture and reason, where the contention seems to be for Truth, and not for Victory) to suffer faire-play on all sides, and to yeeld that liberty to every free borne subject, which (I humbly conceive) the Law of God, of Nature, and this Kingdome gives.

I know it is objected that many dangerous Books come out by my Licence, and that notwithstanding, by mine own acknowledgement, they are different from my judgment. To this I answer

First, *the Books which meet harshest censure, such as the* Bloudy Tenent, *the Treatise about* Divorce, *and others that have Affinity with these, I have been so farre from licensing, that I have not so much as seene or heard of them, till after they have been commonly sold abroad;*

and how many such like I have refused to license, some scores can witness.

Secondly, if sometimes a moderate and useful Discourse, containing things in it differing (happily) from mine own opinion, hath pass'd my hand: yet (as I have already said) the nature and matter of it hath been alwayes such, as did not rationally appeare to me, to carry in it any likelihood of real prejudice, to the propagation of the Gospel, the Authority of Parliament, or the publique peace, but rather an help to discover what before was more darke, if not directly, yet accidentally at least, by putting men upon further search and study in the matters controverted: which sort of Books, whilst I have licensed, I can truly say, that I have done it, as a lover of Truth: and if this be a crime, then I can recriminate; for divers of the other Licensers, (upon the aforesaid grounds, as I charitably conceive) began to take this liberty before mee.

But thirdly and lastly, (that I may give a ful and sufficient answer,) I am ready to offer an account for whatsoever Bookes I have licensed: and because I heare that some of my kind Brethren have been at the cost and paines, to take a Catalogue of Bookes licensed by mee (for what ends themselves best know) I shall also prepare a Catalogue of Bookes, licensed by other hands, which being compared with the bookes of my licensing, let the world judge, who it is, that hath licensed bookes of most dangerous consequence: I am neither afraid nor ashamed in this matter to stand upon my vindication, not doubting of equal dealing from my Judges, viz. that other Licensers, with the bookes licensed by them, shall be examined also. In the mean time, I shall doe my duty, and according to the Trust committed to me by both houses of Parliament, shall endeavour faithfully to serve Christ, in the preservation both of the liberty of Truth, and the sweetnesse of union among Brethren.

Thus farre good Reader, thou art desired to accept an Apology, in case any exceptions should be taken against this or any other piece licensed by

John Bachiler.[18]

Several points in Bachiler's statement deserve special attention. The allusion to the treatise on divorce is not such as would be made by one who had been favorably impressed by *Areopagitica*, or who was on terms of friendly acquain-

---

[18] The italics in the above passage are the editor's. Both Edwards in his *Gangraena* and Vicars in his *Schismatick Sifted* (see above) gave lists of books licensed by Bachiler. No list by Bachiler of books licensed by other hands has come to light.

tance with its author. Bachiler was, as his statement shows, not in marked disagreement from the principles expressed in *Areopagitica*, but he writes as though he had never heard of that work, and knew only the divorce tract, which he links in the usual way with *The Bloudy Tenent*, as a familiar example of a notoriously dangerous book. Far from showing any approval for Milton's tract on freedom of the press, supposing him even to have read it, Bachiler plainly implies that he condemns both the divorce tract and *The Bloudy Tenent*, and that he would have refused to license either book, if the author had applied to him for that purpose.

The evidence of contemporary pamphlets points, therefore, to the following conclusions concerning Milton's reputation and influence in the years immediately following 1643. (1) Little or nothing was known of him to the pamphleteers and the general public, save as the author of a scandalous book which was widely condemned, but not widely read. (2) Since none of the critics of the divorce tract seems to have had any personal knowledge of Milton, even of his marital difficulties, we are led to infer that he refrained from association with any recognized groups of Independents, sectaries or Levellers. (3) *Areopagitica*, perhaps for the reasons suggested above (pages 73-75), seems to have attracted no contemporary attention, and to have had no discernible effect.

We may note finally that at no time was Milton persecuted, as others were, for violation of the printing ordinance. John Goodwin was deprived of his place at St. Stephen's in Coleman Street. Lilburne, Overton and William Larner were thrown in prison. Milton was, to be sure, cited once in the Commons and once in the Lords, but nothing came of the matter in either case. This does not suggest that he was a conspicuous person, or one regarded as particularly dangerous by the Presbyterian extremists.

BIBLIOGRAPHY

BIBLIOGRAPHY

Abbott, W. C., Bibliography of Oliver Cromwell, Cambridge, Mass., 1929.

Arber, Edward, Transcript of the Registers of the Company of Stationers, 1475-1640, London, 1875.

Barclay, Robert, Inner Life of the Religious Societies of the Commonwealth, London, 1876.

> Barclay, Dexter, Neal, and several other works not listed here, deal with the history of particular religious groups, making large use of material drawn from the pamphlet literature. Sectarian bias limits the value even of the best of these books.

Bernstein, Eduard, Sozialismus und Demokratie in der grossen englishchen Revolution, Stuttgart, 1908. Translated as Cromwell and Communism, London, 1930.

> Similarly biased, though the bias is of more recent origin.

Burrage, Champlin, The Early English Dissenters in the Light of Recent Research, Cambridge, 1912.

> Important for its detailed account of the historical literature about the nonconformists and the dissenting sects. Gives a list of the more important collections of books and manuscripts relating to those subjects in this country and in England.

Catalogue of the Pamphlets, Books, Newspapers, and Manuscripts Collected by George Thomason, London, 1908.

> Upon the assembling of the Long Parliament, George Thomason, a London bookseller, began systematically to collect copies of all books and pamphlets appearing at the time in London and, to a certain extent, in other parts of the kingdom. He continued until the coronation of Charles II in 1661. After the first few months, he generally wrote on the title-page of each item the day of the month on which he entered it in his list. The collection, remaining virtually intact after his death, found its way by gift of George III to the library of the British Museum. Though not exhaustive for the period, it is by far the largest collection of the kind, containing upwards of twenty thousand titles. The Catalogue is indispensable but unreliable. Titles are abbreviated without indication. Though they are arranged chronologically by day and month, Thomason's dates are used and cited only when the cataloguer has been unable to find other information. Authority for departing from Thomason's

dates is not given. The index is inaccurate, incomplete, and confused. The Catalogue does not include the considerable number of works of the period not in the Thomason Collection, but contained in the British Museum.

Davies, Godfrey, Bibliography of British History, Stuart Period, Oxford, 1928.

Dexter, H. M., Congregationalism of the Last Three Hundred Years, New York, 1880.

Contains a somewhat inaccurate list of the author's extensive collection of books and pamphlets, now in the library of Yale University.

Dictionary of National Biography, London, 1885-1900.

Particularly the articles by C. H. Firth.

Eyre, G. E. B., Transcript of the Registers of the Company of Stationers, 1640-1708, London, 1913.

Gardiner, S. R., History of the Great Civil War, London, 1893.

Indispensable for a knowledge of events, but far less useful for the history of thought and expression.

Gillett, C. R., Catalogue of the McAlpin Collection, New York, 1927-1930.

The most useful bibliographical tool for dealing with the pamphlets of the period. It lists not less than fifteen thousand titles from 1500 to 1700, in the library of the Union Theological Seminary in New York. The collection is particularly rich in the period 1640-1660, and contains a significant number of items not found in the British Museum.

Gooch, G. P., English Democratic Ideas in the Seventeenth Century, second edition with notes by H. J. Laski, Cambridge, 1927.

In default of a more critical and less summary handling of the material, the most useful review of any considerable amount of the pamphlet literature.

Hanserd Knollys Society, Publications of the, London, 1846-1854.

Harleian Miscellany, The, London, 1808-1813.

This collection, the Somers Tracts, the Publications of the Hanserd Knollys Society, and several others not listed here, reprint pamphlets of the period chiefly interesting for their bearing on political history or on the history of particular religious groups. The selection of works included in these collections is such that they must be used with caution by students of the literature as a whole.

McKerrow, R. B., Dictionary of Printers and Booksellers in England . . . 1557-1640, London, 1910.

Masson, David, Life of John Milton, London, 1877-1896.
  Indispensable for biographical details concerning Milton, but
  its point of view is distorted by hero worship, and it is, Gardiner
  to the contrary notwithstanding, superficial in its treatment of the
  literature concerning liberty of conscience.

Neal, Daniel, History of the Puritans, New York, 1843-1844.

Pease, T. C., The Leveller Movement, Washington, 1916.
  An excellent account of the Levellers after 1647, especially in
  relation to constitutional history and political theory.

Plomer, H. R., Dictionary of Printers and Booksellers in England . . .
  1641-1667, London, 1907.

Shaw, W. A., History of the English Church during the Civil Wars
  and under the Commonwealth, London, 1900.

Somers Tracts, London, 1809-1815.

Tawney, R. H., Religion and the Rise of Capitalism, London, 1926.
  Should be read in conjuction with Weber. Draws its illustrations
  mainly from the literature of the periods immediately preceding
  and following the Civil Wars and the Commonwealth.

Troeltsch, Ernst, Die Sociallehren der christlichen Kirchen und Grup-
  pen, Tübingen, 1912. Translated as The Social Teaching of the
  Christian Churches, New York, 1931.

Weber, Max, Die protestantische Ethik und der Geist des Kapitalis-
  mus, Tübingen, 1904-1905. Translated as The Protestant Ethic
  and the Spirit of Capitalism, London, 1930.
  Probably overstates its case, but is the most stimulating critical
  treatment in recent times of the spiritual significance of Puritanism.

NOTES

5, l. 32   *though*] *through*

9, l. 7   momentany] momentary

   l. 20   sheb] shed

   l. 28   one] on

11, l. 4   rhey] they

   l. 10   *Sarr-Chamber*] *Starr-Chamber*

12, l. 34   *Unmasking the mistery of iniquitie*] Probably refers to *The Mysterie of Iniquitie: That is to say, The Historie of the Papacie*, a translation by Samson Lennard, published in 1612, of Phillipe de Mornay's *Mysterium iniquitatis*. See Brooke's *Discourse*, Vol. II, p. 85 and note. I have found no record of any translation later than that of Lennard nor of any edition of Lennard's translation later than 1612.

13, l. 3   on] one

   l. 29   *Dr. Bastwicks Answer*, and his *Letany*] For *Letany* see Vol. I, pp. 11-13. Bastwick's defence before Star Chamber in 1637 was published as *The Answer of John Bastwick, Doctor of Phisicke To the Information of Sir John Bancks Knight, Atturney Universal*, 1637.

   l. 31   *Certaine answers*] The second and fourth parts of Bastwick's *Letany* 1637 were entitled respectively *The Answer of John Bastwick, Doctor of Phisicke to the exceptions made against his Letany by a learned Gentleman* and *A more Full Answer of John Bastwick, Dr. of Phisick, made to the former exceptions newly propounded by another wellwiller to him, against some expressions in his Letany*.

   l. 32   *The vanity and impiety*] The third part of Bastwick's *Letany* was entitled *The Vanity and Mischief of the Old Letany*.

   l. 34   *A Breviat*] Prynne, *A Breviate of the Prelates intolerable usurpations both upon the kings Prerogative Royall, and the Subjects Liberties*, 1635.

   l. 35   *16. new Queries*] Prynne, *XVI. New Quaeres Proposed to our Lord Praelates*, 1637.

14, l. 1   on] one

l. 14   his *Flagellum* . . . and his *Apologeticus*] See above, Vol. I, p. 10.

15, l. 1   *Mr. Nicholas Fuller*] Nicholas Fuller (1543-1620), barrister of Gray's Inn, published in 1607 *The Argument of Master Nicholas Fuller in the Case of Thomas Lad, and Richard Maunsell, his Clients. Wherein it is plainly proved, that the Ecclesiasticall Commissioners have no power, by vertue of their Commission, to Imprison, to put to the Oath Ex Officio, or to fine any of his Majesties Subjects.* Reprinted 1641.

16, l. 34   discirbed] discribed   yon] you

17, l. 8   *Pocklingtons* Booke] Richard Pocklington (d. 1642), chaplain to the Bishop of Lincoln, published *Sunday No Sabbath*, 1636, and *Altare Christianum*, 1637. The latter was attacked by Prynne in *A Quench-Coale*, 1637, together with other books "calling the Lords Table an Altar, or placing it Altar-wise." In 1641 Parliament received a *Petition and Articles* against Pocklington as "a chief author and ring-leader in all those innovations which have of late flowed into the Church of England." He was deprived by the Lords (February 12, 1641) of all preferments, and the two books above-mentioned were ordered burnt in the City of London and in the two universities by the common hangman.

18, l. 24   mals] makes

l. 26   thē] them   vē] even   mē] men

19, l. 3   coulors] coulors;

24, l. 24   one] on

25, l. 20   on] one

26, l. 6   *though*] *through*

27, l. 25   afrer] after

28. l. 28   businesses . . . concerning *Dr. Laiton* and *Mr. Burton*] Adequate surveillance of political prisoners was in the seventeenth century difficult to maintain. Leighton and Burton had exasperated the authorities by circumventing the vigilance of the Warden of the Fleet. Consequently Lilburne was handled with particular rigor. Alexander Leighton (1568-1649), physician and divine, was arrested February 17, 1630, for the publication in 1628 of a petition to Parliament against prelacy which he had expanded into a book and printed in Holland, *An Appeal To the Parliament, Or Sions Plea against the Prelacie.* Condemned by Star Chamber to be

whipt, pilloried and shorn of his ears, he escaped from the Fleet before sentence could be executed against him. He was recaptured, subjected to the punishment prescribed, and imprisoned once more in the Fleet, whence he was released by Parliament in 1640. See his *Epitome*, 1646. Henry Burton had been put into the Fleet for a short time in 1629 because of his *Babel no Bethel*. The events leading to his later imprisonment have been recounted above. While in the Fleet before his trial with Prynne and Bastwick in Star Chamber in June, 1637, he added to his offence by publishing *An Apology of an Appeale*, 1636, consisting of epistles to the king, the judges, and "the true-hearted nobility."

29, l. 19 *Flagelluw*] *Flagellum*

33, l. 23 rhey] they

41, l. 9 *Retirements . . . in the last Recesse*] Parliament took a recess September 9, 1641, upon the king's going to Scotland. It reassembled October 20, 1641.

50, l. 10 our] their. See Errata, p. 44.

51, l. 31 himselfe, yet)] himselfe,) yet

52, l. 39 *Cloppenburge*] Johannes Cloppenburg or Jean Everhardt Cloppenburch (1592-1652), a Dutch theologian, published his *Sacrificiorum patriarchalium schola sacra* in 1637.

57, l. 1 the,] the

65, l. 16 Master *Ball*] John Ball (1586-1640), a non-conformist divine opposed to separation, author of *A Friendly Triall Of the Grounds Tending to Separation*, 1640.

66, ll. 15-21 So that at . . . was said before.] The first edition reads: And now this case comes not to our question, which is of the *Best* in all circumstances; for wee know one circumstance may so alter the case, that now *That* may be *worst, which else* would have beene *best*, as was said before. So that at this time, *This* cannot be *Better* than *That*, except *This* be not onely in it selfe *expedient*, but also *more* expedient than *That* is at this present: for one graine of more *expedience* makes that to be *Best*, which else would be *Worst*.

67, l. 18 tkey] they

74, l. 39 to] so

80, l. 12 R. Ea. of E.] Robert Earl of Essex

83, l. 25 bue] but

85, l. 1 *Broughtons* Epistle] Hugh Broughton (1549-1612), divine and scholar, wrote a number of pamphlets against the Roman Church, to one of which Brooke is doubtless here alluding.

l. 2   *Nichol. de Clémengiis*] Nicolas de Clémanges, born about 1360, rector of the University of Paris, was active in the effort to end the schism in the western church. He is credited with having written *De corrupto ecclesiae statu*, an attack on the morality and discipline of the church, first edited by Cordatus (probably Ulrich von Hutten) in 1513. Hence he is sometimes regarded as a reformer of the type of Wycliff and Huss. It is now generally believed, however, that the *De corrupto ecclesiae statu* was written not by de Clémanges but by some contemporary in the faculty of the University of Paris.

l. 3   that Noble Learned Lords] Philippe de Mornay (1549-1623), Seigneur du Plessis-Marly, was a French Protestant, a Huguenot apologist and diplomat. He represented Henry of Navarre in England in 1577-78, in 1580, and was sent on a mission to Queen Elizabeth in 1592. He was the author of *Mysterium iniquitatis, seu historia papatus* 1611, dedicated to James I. This was translated in 1612 by Samson Lennard and published as *The Mysterie of Iniquitie: That is to say, The Historie of the Papacie*. I have been unable to trace the "late prints" in which, according to Brooke, de Mornay's work had been expurgated. See above, p. 12 note.

101, l. 23 asd] and

102, l. 3   Manner of all Ordinances] all Manner of Ordinances

103, l. 25   *Du Plessis*] See above, p. 85 note.

110, l. 3   a most Reverend man] Joseph Hall (1574-1656), Bishop of Exeter, later of Norwich. The reference is to his *Episcopacie By Divine Right Asserted*. See above Vol. I, p. 16.

116, l. 16   *Downham*] George Downham or Downame (d. 1634), Bishop of Derry, Calvinist, came into conflict with Laud over the latter's Arminianism in 1631. He had previously defended the divine institution of episcopacy in *A Sermon defending the honourable function of Bishops*, published 1609, and *A Defence Of the Sermon Preached at the Consecration of the Bishop of Bath and Welles*, 1611. It is to the two latter works that Brooke refers. *Bilson*] Thomas Bilson (1546/7-1616), Bishop of Worcester, later of Winchester, wrote in 1585 at Elizabeth's request *The True Difference Betweene Christian Subjection and Unchristian Rebel-*

lion, defending the English Church against the Catholics. He was also the author of *The Perpetual Government of Christes Church*, 1593, second edition 1610, to which Brooke here refers.   one of their owne] Bishop Joseph Hall. See above, p. 110 note.

117, l. 24 *Thorndick*] Herbert Thorndike (1598-1672), scholar and theologian, appointed Hebrew lecturer at Trinity College, Cambridge, in October, 1640, later active in editing the Syriac portion of Walton's *Polyglott*, was the author of *Of the Government Of Churches; a discourse Pointing at the Primitive Form* 1641, to which Brooke here refers.

l. 37 Prebyter] Presbyter. See Errata, p. 44 above.

126, l. 16 Who is meant . . . *be to thee*.] The first edition reads: Who is meant by *Them v.* 17. (if hee will not heare them.)

133, l. 5 *Mead*] Joseph Mead or Mede (1586-1638), fellow of Christ's College, Cambridge, was well known as a biblical scholar and man of encyclopedic learning. He was particularly famous for his *Clavis apocalyptica*, 1627. Brooke here refers to his *The Apostasy Of The Latter Times*, 1641.

134, l. 33 *Family of Love*, the *Antinomians*, and *Grindletonians*] See above, Vol. I, pp. 42-44.

137, l. 36 *Book of Sports*] *The Declaration of Sports*, authorizing the people to engage in sports and pastimes on Sunday after services, was commanded (1618) by James to be read in all churches in the kingdom, to the great scandal of all persons of Puritan sympathies.

141, l. 22 letting] setting. See Errata, p. 44 above.

150, l. 13 presse

153, l. 26 One poor discourse of *Truth*] For Brooke's essay on *The Nature of Truth* see Vol. I, p. 20.

155, l. 6 it is] is it

156, l. 36 *Oiders*] Orders

159, l. 30 pefect] perfect

l. 36 Yet *Light* was on] The first edition reads: Light was one of

160, ll. 22-33 But why doe . . . against the Spirit.] The first edition reads: Godly men may not onely neglect, but abuse light; Yea they may both *grieve*, and *quench* Gods Holy *Spirit*. A sad case! yet are they not still in some part *Carnall*? and the *Flesh* not onely lusteth, but warreth against the *Spirit*.

162, l. 3 pirit] spirit

l. 7 pro e] prove

169, l. 13   the late bills] Charles assented June 22, 1641, to a bill which terminated the tonnage and poundage duties and by which he surrendered forever the right to levy customs duties of any kind without the consent of Parliament. On July 5, 1641, he assented to bills abolishing the Courts of Star Chamber and High Commission.

176, l. 15   3 of *November* 1640] The date of the assembling of the Long Parliament.

177, l. 37   Strafford] Thomas Wentworth, Earl of Strafford, Lord Lieutenant of Ireland and Charles I's principal minister at the time of the assembling of the Long Parliament, was the prime object of popular hatred in 1640. He was impeached by the House of Commons on the charge that he had "endeavoured to subvert the fundamentall laws and government of the realms of England and Ireland" and substitute for them arbitrary and tyrannical government. His trial began March 23 and his execution occurred May 12, 1641.

178, l. 20   Militia and the Magazine of Hull] At the moment at which Parker was writing, the bitter controversy between the king and the Parliament concerning Hull was raging. In January, 1642, Charles took measures to secure his personal control of Hull in order to gain possession of the munitions stored there and the use of the port for bringing in forces which the queen was attempting to raise abroad. Parliament ordered Sir John Hotham to secure the city and not to deliver it up except by "the King's authority, signified unto him by the Lords and Commons now assembled in Parliament." Charles, regarding the appointment of Hotham as an illegal act, proceeded to Hull April 23 with a small force and attempted to enter. Hotham refused him admission to the town, and was immediately proclaimed a traitor by the king. The incident, universally regarded as the first overt clash pointing to the imminence of war, was the subject of acrimonious discussion in the pamphlets of the moment.

186, l. 26   Pople] People

191, l. 10   two contrary armies] In 1639 the troubles of Charles I came to a head in his attempt to impose the Book of Common Prayer on the Scotch Church at the instance of Laud and the Anglican party. The king assembled an army and marched to the border only to draw back in the face of the Scottish forces assembled on Dunse

Law. In 1640, after dissolving the Short Parliament, Charles made another futile attempt to overcome Scottish resistance by force of arms. On this occasion, however, the Scotch army crossed the border and compelled the confused forces of the king to withdraw from Newcastle. The Scotch continued to hold Newcastle pending the settlement of issues which promptly arose upon the assembling of the Long Parliament.

192, l. 5   at reasonable] a treasonable

193, l. 4   Militia] During the early months of 1642, the rivalry between the king and Parliament came to an issue in the argument over a bill for establishing a national militia. Parliament sought to secure to itself control over this force by vesting the command in a lord general to be named in the act itself. This was opposed by the king, who sought to retain military power in his own hands. After several futile attempts at compromise, Parliament finally in April set up machinery for establishing train bands in the counties under the command of persons named by itself. Charles's attempt to prohibit the execution of this act came to nothing.

198, l. 34   stirres and tumults] The debates of Parliament in the closing months of 1641 and the early months of 1642 were frequently attended by more or less riotous assemblages of citizens outside the royal palace of Whitehall and the doors of Westminster Hall, where Parliament assembled. These tumults were the occasion, in the opinion of the popular party, for various attempts on the part of the court party to overawe Parliament by force. On December 29, 1641, a number of Cavaliers, encountering a crowd of citizens who were crying out against popish lords and bishops under the windows of the palace, drew their swords and precipitated an affray in the street, in which several persons appear to have been injured.

199, l. 20   five members] The reference is to Charles's breach of the privilege of Parliament in invading the floor of the House of Commons in his unsuccessful attempt of January 3 and 4, 1642, to arrest Pym, Hampden, Holles, Hazelrigg and Strode, members of the house.

200, l. 25   *Hooker*

205, l. 24   over] ever

206, l. 7   more

211, l. 35   Himself, and the Kingdom] Himself and the Kingdom

230, l. 26   pre end] pretend

236, l. 7   Doctors) still object and reply] Doctors still object and reply)

244, l. 11   designe of bringing up the Army] In March, 1641, there was fear in Parliamentary circles lest pressure might be brought to bear upon them by the army which Charles had assembled in the north for that futile attack on the Scots which had resulted in the calling of the Long Parliament and negotiations for paying the Scottish army to go home. Proposals seem to have been made to induce the officers to sign a declaration in support of the king and the bishops. A bolder proposal was made by Sir John Suckling and Henry Jermyn to put Goring in command and march on London. In the confusion of counsel about the king, nothing came of these proposals.

247, l. 5   bucthers] butchers

249, l. 24   never] never have

l. 30   that] that are

255, l. 12   substanee] substance

258, l. 28   bow] how

264, l. 1   on] or

266, l. 33   hsnds] hands

282(7), l. 14   un-] unto

289(22), l. 6   It it] It is

l. 23   affirmed

301(45), l. 9   they] the Anabaptists, Brownists and Separatists

304, l. 1   ous] our

315, l. 7   some of our brethren in their printed bookes] The note in the margin referring to Mr. Cheynett should read: Cheynell. Francis Cheynell, an active Presbyterian clergyman and member of the Westminster Assembly, in his *Rise, Growth, and Danger of Socinianisme* (May 24), 1643, well illustrates the confusion that resulted from the effort to make the alignment of men on questions of religious doctrine and church government exactly correspond to their alignment on intellectual and political questions. The Apologists, standing like the Brownists and other dissenters for the independency of congregations, nevertheless repudiated the Brownists and regarded themselves as loyal to the English Church. Cheynell in his zeal to combat the oncoming of rationalism, which he denominates Socinianism, lumps both "the Arminian, Socinian

and Popish Party" and "the Atheists, Anabaptists and Sectaries."
Yet he is at pains to show that not all nonconformists are to be
condemned. He admits that some Independent ministers, sometimes put down for Brownists if not Anabaptists, have been willing to "communicate even in a Parish-Assembly and have publicly
protested against Brownism." He refers at this point to "Mr.
Thomas Goodwin his Fast Sermon preached at Westminster,"
saying "I heard the same man preach since with much fervency
and earnestnesse against the Brownists." (*Rise, Growth and
Danger of Socinianisme*, p. 65.)

l. 30   *Guiciardine*] Francesco Guicciardini (1483-1540), Italian
historian and statesman, served three popes from 1515 to 1534 in
important positions connected with the government of the papal
states, and then served the Medici until 1537. He spent his last
years in the composition of his *Storia d'Italia*, which dealt with the
period 1494-1532 and which was translated into most European
languages. Guicciardini hated the papacy and attributed the woes
of Italy to the ambitions of the church.

320, l. 32   *Cartwright*, holy *Baynes*] *Thomas Cartwright* (1535-
1603), student and professor at Cambridge, was the head of the
Puritan party in the controversies over church government under
Elizabeth. He advocated a Presbyterian system of church discipline
and organization.
Paul Baynes (d. 1617), famous for his piety, was a Puritan divine,
at one time fellow of Christ's College, Cambridge, who suffered
persecution and deprivation of his livings in the church by reason
of his non-conformist teachings.

331, l. 23   Schime] Schism

VOLUME III

10, l. 7   defeat at *Newark*] Newark, besieged by Parliamentary
forces, was relieved by Prince Rupert March 22, 1644.

17, l. 37   *Gualter*] Goodwin quotes in the margin from Rudolph
Gaulter (1519-1586), Swiss theologian and exegetist: "Interim
oraculi instar nobis esse debet, quòd Dei consilia nullis hominum
viribus impedire posse humana verò suá sponte collabi discimus,
Homil. 37 in Act."

23, l. 37   interprepation] interpretation
l. 38   sgainst] against

24, l. 7   Author] Author of

49, ll. 15-37   Fourthly (and lastly) . . . I answer,] Fourthly (and
lastly) the gracious and bountifull God hath so laid it in his counsell and decree, that, though the saying be true, which our Saviour
taketh notice of, *Joh.* 4.37. *That one soweth, and another reapeth;*
yet *both he that soweth, and he that reapeth, should reioyce together.* ver. 36 So that as *Abigail* told *David,* that *when the Lord
should have done unto him all the good which he had promised him,
it would be no grief unto him, nor offence of mind, that he had not
shed blood causelesse, or avenged himself*; no more will it be the
least occasion of uncomfortablenesse or complaint unto Ministers,
who have been faithfull unto God, and brought home souls unto
him, when *they shall shine like stars in the firmament of Heaven,*
that some of the children of their labours departed from under their
hand when time was, to seek pasture and soul-accomodations elsewhere.

Another objection seeming to war with an high hand against the
way hitherto protected, is this: Can that in reason be thought to be
the *way* of God, which seemeth so onely in the eyes of a few incon-
siderable, and (for the most part) illiterate persons? and not rather
that, which triumpheth in the vote and suffrage of a Reverend,
learned, pious and frequent Assembly; yea and further hath the
approbation of many wise and worthy persons in full concurrence
with it? Do not wise men see more then those that are weak, and
many, then few? I answer,

50, l. 36   *11th] all the*

54, l. 34   learned Gentleman] William Prynne, *Independency Examined, Unmasked, Refuted* (September 26), 1644. See Vol. I, p. 51.
l. 36   two Brethren of this Way] *A Reply of two of the Brethren . . . Formerly called M.S. to A.S.* (July 11), 1644. See Vol. I,
p. 52.

62(ii), l. 5   Peolpe] People have
63(v), l. 20   *hento] then to*
64(vi), l. 2   uncough] uncouth
65(1), l. 2   Apologeticall Narration] See Vol. I, pp. 46-52, Vol. II,
pp. 306-337.
66(3), l. 20   assistane] assistance
l. 21   eheir] their
68(7), l. 17   *Enthusiasmas*

(8), l. 17   abe] able

71(13), l. 13   be it instanced] be instanced

l. 20   fit (to] (fit to

73(18), ll. 20-22   break, out euen against their owne interest. Nay some say further, that they did well indeed in being so zealous against

76(23), l. 11   with] which

77(25), l. 1   repetions] repetitions

(26), l. 4   more

l. 12   easie

l. 20   a lwyes] alwayes

81(33), l. 5   presumptfious] presumptuous

l. 19   perver ed] perverted

82(35), l. 10   artificiall

ll. 19-23   Liberty of the Subject on the other side; yet both of these mainely intend their owne respective profits, and advancements; so that which side soever prevaile

84(40), l. 4   scandalous] (scandalous

85(41), l. 12   bencfeiall] beneficiall

(42), l. 18   wicked *Procrustes*

86(44), l. 9   *Ob.* Nothing is more dangerous] This objection to his own argument which Walwyn poses for rebuttal, together with the two similar ensuing objections, are directly derived from *Certaine Considerations to Dis-swade Men from further gathering of Churches* (December 28), 1643. This was put forth by the five Apologists and fifteen other members of the Assembly. By "gathering of Churches" was meant the formation of sects or congregations of worshipers outside of and by implication in opposition to the authority of the parish churches of the persons thus involved. A summary of the significant points of the pamphlet, to which Walwyn is from here on closely referring, will indicate the very conservative nature of the Apologists' conception of toleration. It is said to belong "to Christian magistrates in an especiall manner to be authorizers of, and Ministers of the Gospel to be leaders in" the reformation of the Church. While they are doing this, the people should "encourage them, joyne with them and wait upon them." Parliament and the Assembly are at this time fulfilling that very function. Since Satan is attempting "to destroy the Parliament, and cause this worke of God to cease; nothing can be more destructive to the friends of the cause of Religion, then to be divided among themselves." "That therefore all Ministers and people be earnestly entreated to forbeare for a convenient time the joyning of themselves into Church-societies of any kind whatsoever, untill they see whether the right Rule will not bee commended to them in this orderly way." "While men are in expectation that a way according to their consciences may be approved or allowed of by the Magistrates, it is unfit and will bee uncomfortable, beforehand to provoke by setting up their owne." "If after all their waiting, the right rule should not bee delivered unto them, and they then called to suffer (which wee hope will never be) for doing what shall appeare to be their dutie, they shall have the more peace with God, and their conscience, while they shall witnesse with them that to present occasions of divisions they abstained not onely from what was sinfull, but even from what was by them judged to bee lawfull whilst unseasonable."

87(46), l. 18   cotntenanced] countenanced
88(47), l. 10   poselites] proselites
93(57), l. 11   wrethed] wretched
94(59), l. 13   beleife
  (60), l. 12   ssrenght] strength
       l. 19   ssupect] suspect
95(62), l. 1   owne tenets, or know
       l. 5   goe
       l. 8   sportfull
       l. 18   short a
96(63), l. 21   Ordieances] Ordinances
99(70), l. 6   *Confutation of Anabaptists*] Thomas Bakewell, *A Confutation of the Anabaptists, and All others who affect not Civill Government* (June 21), 1644. See Vol. I, pp. 61, 124, 125.
       l. 18   of time
100(71), l. 18   *History of the Anabaptists*] *A Warning for England Especially for London In The Famous History of the Frantick Anabaptists Their wild Preachings and Practices in Germany* (February) 1642.
101(73), l. 17   ahat] that
  (74), l. 1   should in their
       l. 9   to given] to be given
102(75), l. 5   *Wrens* Conformity] Matthew Wren (1585-1667),

Bishop successively of Hereford, Norwich and Ely, was notorious
among the Puritans for the vigor of his effort to enforce the policies
of Laud in the Church and for his persecution of non-conformists.
He was attacked by Prynne in *Newes from Ipswich*, 1636 (see
above, Vol. I, p. 10). He was confined by Parliament in the Tower
from 1641 to 1660.

   l. 7 prerend] pretend

   l. 18 altering

103(78), l. 23 the 35. of *Eliz.*] Parliament passed a law in 1593 providing that those who wilfully abstained from church for a month
and actively impugned the ecclesiastical authority of the crown, or
persuaded others to abstain from church, or attended or persuaded
others to attend unlawful conventicles, should be liable to imprisonment until they submitted, and if they did not submit within three
months, that they were to abjure the realm and be treated as felons
if they returned.

108, l. 27 *Aulicus*] *Mercurius Aulicus* was the Royalist rival to the
Parliamentary news-sheet, *Mercurius Brittanicus*. It was issued at
Oxford by Sir John Birkenhead daily from January 8, 1643, to
September 7, 1645, and occasionally after that, in order to com-
municate "the intelligence and affairs of the court to the rest of the
kingdom."

109, l. 24 forced

   l. 25 abolished

110, l. 31 mangage] manage

112, l. 39 *Classis*

115, l. 2 desire

   l. 13 leave

   l. 26 condition

120, l. 17 perish] persist. See Errata, p. 116.

122, l. 13 ingenious] ingenuous. See Errata, p. 116.

   l. 38 *Barbaria*] Barbery. See Errata, p. 116.

125, l. 12 was] was many times. See Errata, p. 116.

126, l. 20 perish] persist. See Errata, p. 116.

128, l. 22 where] whence. See Errata, p. 116.

129, l. 35 ambitious] ambitions

130, l. 27 these] those. See Errata, p. 116.

134, l. 34 ingenious] ingenuous. See Errata, p. 116.

136, l. 5 besides] besides doubting. See Errata, p. 116.

138, l. 14 I answer] I make answer. See Errata, p. 116.

140, l. 39 sit] sit one. See Errata, p. 116.

141, l. 32 what

l. 37 will] will not

143, l. 1 In a Sermon] A note in the margin refers to "Mr. Alexander Hendersons Ser. pag. 18." The sermon referred to was published in 1644 as *A Sermon preached to the Honourable House of Commons . . . December 27, 1643*.

144, l. 32 expressively] expressely. See Errata, p. 116.

l. 41 the words] these words

145, l. 2 possibly cannot] cannot possibly. See Errata, p. 116.

146, l. 29 which] with. See Errata, p. 116.

148, l. 14 made] make. See Errata, p. 116.

149, l. 11 apprehending] apprehended. See Errata, p. 116.

155, l. 20 be they

163, ll. 15-23 *hesaies . . . Magist. puniendis*] See Errata, p. 116. The passage should probably read as follows: "he saies, God never gave power to man for imposing Lawes upon the Conscience, nor can endure that anybody besides himselfe should beare sway or dominion over the mindes of men, And *Beza*, Though he write a whole tract about punishing of Heretickes, yet he could not chuse but acknowledge so much truth in a few lines only as confutes the whole Treatise, where he tells us, That as the Church has no power of forcing of its owne, so neither may it require such of civill Magistrates, to imploy it in a coercive way: *de Haeret. à Civil. Magist. puniendis*."

165, l. 22 extraordinary] extraordinarily. See Errata, p. 116.

l. 29 as] us. See Errata, p. 116.

l. 38 principalls] principles

166, l. 12 for the] for your. See Errata, p. 116.

l. 27 as yet] as is yet. See Errata, p. 116.

167, l. 41 then] rather than. See Errata, p. 116.

171, l. 20 have] have not. See Errata, p. 116.

172, l. 6 principalls] principles. See Errata, p. 116.

174, l. 10 hate the light

182, ll. 1-6 I have found them full of bitter and unsavoury Language against the poore Saints of God, and the unspotted wais of Jesus Christ, and finding your Confidence very great but your Arguments very weake and unsound (having received a Talent from the Lord,

I conceived myselfe bound in Conscience to imploy it, and lay it out for my Masters best advantage) and I was determined

l. 9   *Blacke-Coate?*] *Blacke-Coates*

l. 16   partilulars] particulars

l. 20   promoting

l. 24   *Syodianlike*] *Synodianlike*

183, l. 3   *Imrpimatur*] *Imprimatur*

l. 8   print so fast

l. 15   *have about*] *have a bout*

184, l. 9   *thir*] *this*

186, ll. 1-2   *Religion they please*, or may mould it to the maners of their people; so that Queen *Mary*

187, ll. 6-7   *to to*] *to do*

l. 10   Common Prayer . . . Tythes] On January 4, 1645, the Lords finally accepted the Commons' amendments to the ordinance which abolished the Book of Common Prayer and set up instead the Presbyterian Directory of Worship, published March 13, 1645. For the Ordinance for Tythes see Vol. I, p. 77.

193, l. 35   Romes master-piece; and the Archbishops Diary] Prynne's *Romes Master-Peece* (31 May) 1643 asserted that the civil wars in England and Scotland were caused by the grand conspiracy of the Pope to extirpate Protestantism in England. Walwyn is arguing that, if this were true, then Prynne inconsistently displays Laud at enmity with the Catholics. Laud's journal was published by Prynne as *A Breviate of the Life of William Laud Arch-bishop of Canterbury: Extracted . . . out of his owne Diary*, 1644. See Vol. I, p. 11.

194, l. 12   fiend] feind [feigned]

l. 35   *Selden*] John Selden (1584-1654), jurist, antiquarian, legal writer, orientalist, lay member of the Westminster Assembly and one of the most learned men of the time, was the author of *The History of Tythes*, 1618, in which he endeavored to prove that the exaction of tithes by the church was not *jure divino*.

l. 39   value

195, l. 22   and the weale of all peaceable

196, l. 36   *and of that nature*] *are of that nature*

197, ll. 8-11   *Goodwin . . . Burton*] this paragraph as a whole is devoted to the consideration of Prynne's *Truth Triumphing*, which attempted to vindicate the jurisdiction and coercive power of

"Christian Emperors, Kings, Magistrates, Parliaments, in all matters of Religion." In the same work Prynne went on to attack Goodwin's *Innocencies Triumph* (see Vol. I, pp. 52-53) and Burton's *Vindication of Churches*, 1644, a reply to Prynne's *Independency Examined* and *Twelve Considerable Serious Questions*.

l. 46   that] than that

198, l. 6   *Immedicabile vulnus ense*] Prynne concludes his *Independency Examined* by saying that whatever church discipline Parliament approves must be submitted to "as to a Government, Discipline, Ordinance approved by God; and if any Heretickes, False Teachers, Schismaticks obstinately refuse conformity, after due admonition, and all good means used to reclaim them, the *Poets Divinity* and *Policy* must then take place, as well in Ecclesiasticall as civill and natural maladies:

Cuncta prius tentanda, sed immedicabile vulnus
Ense Rescidendum est, ne pars syncera trahatur."
                                        Ovid *Met.* I, 190-91

l. 27   *fiat justitia*] In the dedicatory epistle to Parliament of his *Truth Triumphing*, after the description of Goodwin here referred to, Prynne warns Parliament against the Independents' scorn of its ecclesiastical supremacy, saying, "Farre be it from my thoughts to exasperate Your *Power* or *Justice* against any *Delinquents* of this Kind; some whereof are so neare and deare unto mee, that it is my heaviest affliction to mention their *extravagancies* in this kind. Of which I trust they (and all their followers) will now be ashamed, and a *Brotherly Admonition* to their Persons (though their Writings undergoe the sharper Censure) will I hope induce them, upon Second thoughts, both to discerne, lament, recant their forementioned *Paradoxes*, and abhorre themselves for them even in dust and ashes, (as one of them *professeth hee will doe, in case hee be convinced*). And then if they will not be reclaimed, *Fiat Justitia*, better some should suffer, than all perish."

l. 29   *Bonners* or *Gardiners*] Edmund Bonner or Boner (1500[?]-1569) was consecrated Bishop of London under Henry VIII in 1540. Himself persecuted and imprisoned under Edward VI, he resumed his see in 1553 when Mary ascended the throne and was perforce responsible for the persecutions in the diocese of London from 1554 to 1558.

Stephen Gardiner (1483[?]-1555), consecrated Bishop of Winchester in 1531, was imprisoned under Edward VI and released by Mary and appointed Lord High Chancellor (1553). With Bonner, he has generally been held responsible for the severities of Mary's reign.

209, l. 1   It is decreed] Burgess, Roborough and Byfield were active Presbyterians, prominent members of the Westminster Assembly. For Edwards, author of *Gangraena*, see Vol. I, pp. 80-82.

212, l. 17   12 Articles] In September, 1644, the Presbyterian clergy of the City of London submitted a petition to the House of Commons, begging that the Directory of Worship be expedited and that "erroneous opinions, ruinating schisms, and damnable heresies" be suppressed. The House, at this time dominated by the Presbyterians, passed a vote of thanks to the petitioners (September 18), and Prynne published his *Twelve Considerable Serious Questions*, to which Overton is probably referring.

214, l. 14   *When*] *Wheat*
      l. 37   *Notionall-strength*] *Nationall-strength*

216, l. 29   *peare*] *peace*
      l. 31   *is*] *as*

218, l. 8   propose . . . better] propose those (if no better
      l. 9   Spanish Inquisition
      l. 36   Glosse

221, l. 21   *Lombs*] *Limbs*
      l. 35   love another] love one another

222, l. 15   then to bind

223, l. 20   *Iakce*] *Iacke* [*Jack*]

225, l. 39   not yet
      l. 40   *devoure*: So

226, l. 26   *Calamy*] Edmund Calamy was one of the authors of the *Answer* of Smectymnuus to Bishop Hall's *Remonstrance*, a member of the Westminster Assembly, and one of the most active Presbyterian clergymen and pamphleteers. A late convert to nonconformity, he was one of the most bitter opponents of Independency.

227, l. 2   the arme of flesh suppresse the *cry*

228, l. 1   *intertainement*
      l. 11   *your ne*] *your owne*
      l. 28   *is*] *if*

230, l. 2   Cotton] For John Cotton's *Letter* . . . *to Mr. Williams*, see Vol. I, p. 58. His *Keyes of the Kingdom of Heaven* appeared June 14, 1644.

231, l. 37   thy say] they say

232, l. 4   Cours] Court

234, l. 1   courcive] coercive

l. 4   is to be] it is to be

l. 20   to beene] to have beene

235, l. 24   *to adored*] *to be adored*

236, l. 6   *Iustas Conformity*] This refers to Mr. William Prynne of Lincoln's Inn Esquire, as he generally styled himself on the title-pages of his pamphlets.

237, l. 21   Spear] sphear

l. 36   if all] of all

238, l. 22   *Politians*] *Polititians*

l. 25   and and] and at

242, l. 12   Mr. *Compas. Sam.*] An allusion to Walwyn's anonymous tract, *The Compassionate Samaritane.* See below, l. 27.

l. 20   pap. 4] pag. 4

l. 24   Mr. *Truth-&-Peace*] An allusion to Roger Williams' anonymous tract, *The Bloudy Tenent,* which is couched as a dialogue between Truth and Peace.

243, l. 2   is it preserve] is it to preserve

l. 20   sencence] sentence

244, l. 16   Persent] Present

245, l. 20   the better] the better to

246, l. 10   intringe] infringe

248, l. 20   not ventured] not have ventured

l. 21   Wo] We

249, l. 7   Conquest of *Yorke*] By the victory of Marston Moor, July 2, 1644, the Parliamentary army compelled the Royalists to surrender York and completed the conquest of the north.

l. 23   *bewers*] *bowers*

l. 34   they so aime at, that

l. 39   notwithstanding   subtility our Divines] subtilty of our Divines

250, l. 11   400. and 50. l.] Parliament ordered that this sum be paid to the Westminster Assembly upon submission of the Directory of Worship.

l. 18   mickle Army] Overton is here and elsewhere twitting the

Presbyterians on their repeatedly disappointed hope that the Scots army would take some action that would enable them to control the political situation and enforce Presbyterianism.

251, l. 26   *understand* ;] *understanding*

l. 33   Mr. William] William Prynne.

252, l. 37   as there in] The second edition reads: as those

ll. 39-41   And as for . . . of his prison:] the second edition reads: And as for the good service Justice Conformity mentioned that he performed in his road from Scotland to London, it was so good that the Prisoners there care for no more of his goodnesse.

254, l. 39   *Henry the eight, is Chappell*] The Westminster Assembly met in the Chapel of Henry VII in Westminster Abbey.   *is*] *his*

255, l. 28   Ordinance for Tythes] In spite of bitter opposition from the sects and other radicals, Parliament supported the established system and adopted, November 6, 1644, an "ordinance for the due payment of tithes and such other duties according to the laws and customs of the realm." See Vol. I, p. 77.

259, l. 16   the Booke] *An Exact Collection of all Remonstrances, Declarations, Votes, Orders, Ordinances, Proclamations, Petitions, Messages, Answers, and other Remarkable Passages betweene the Kings most Excellent Majesty, and his High Court of Parliament beginning at his Majesties return from Scotland, being in December 1641, and continued untill March the 21, 1643, 1643.*

260, l. 5   is originall] its originall

l. 7   substance

262, l. 22   last] last but one. See Errata, p. 305.

263, l. 2   that] and that. See Errata, p. 305.

l. 7   the same] for the same. See Errata, p. 305.

264. l. 18   Sir John Lenthall] Sir John Lenthall, keeper of the King's Bench prison, was the brother of William Lenthall, Speaker of the House in the Long Parliament. The Surrey and Salters Hall committees of citizens entered upon an examination of their conduct and in July, 1645, charged them with forwarding £60,000 from Sir Basil Brooke in London to the king at Oxford. Upon report by the Committee of Examinations, the House agreed with that committee that there was no proof of such treasonable action on the part of the Lenthalls, that it was a breach of the privilege of Parliament in the Surrey and Salters Hall committees to enter upon any examination touching the Speaker, and that "Wm. Pendred,

Edward Jenks, and Hanna his Wife, James Freeze, and Stephen
Spratt, have been the principle Instigators and Prosecutors of these
proceedings: and deserve severe and examplary Punishment." Lilburne was put into custody in July, 1645, on the charge of Colonel
King and Bastwick that he had repeated the charges against the
Speaker. Sir John Lenthall was notoriously corrupt and extor-
tionate as keeper of the King's Bench prison, and reputed to have
great influence with his brother, but the evidence is insufficient to
prove that the Speaker himself was corrupt.

265, l. 6   Sir John Hotham] Sir John Hotham, son of John Hotham,
sheriff of Yorkshire, represented Beverly in all five Parliaments of
Charles I and in January, 1642, refused on Parliament's behalf to
surrender Hull to the king. Though anxious for a settlement between king and Parliament, and sympathetic only with the Puritan
desire for civil liberty, he continued to serve Parliament and recovered Scarborough from the Royalists in March, 1643. By the
end of April, however, he was in correspondence with the Earl of
Newcastle, the Royalist commander, concerning the terms on
which a settlement might be brought about. While he was still
negotiating, he was forced to declare himself by the arrest of his
son on charges of misconduct and desertion in battle. The younger
Hotham had involved himself even more deeply with Newcastle.
Before Sir John could admit the Royalist forces to Hull, the town
was seized by the Lord Mayor. Hotham himself was presently
taken and sent to London, brought to the bar of the House September 7, 1643, expelled from his seat and sent to the Tower. He and
his son were condemned to death and executed in January, 1645.
l. 37   Hence justly] And justly   *Parliament* may not] *Parliament* may. See Errata, p. 305.

266, l. 32   Monopolisers] On November 9, 1640, the Commons ordered that all monopolists be excluded from the House, though
complaints were afterwards made that some escaped through favor.
l. 38   Preaching of the Word] On November 15, 1644, the Commons resolved that no person should be allowed to preach unless
ordained in some recognized church.

267, l. 17   *Merchant Adventurers*] The Merchant Adventurers were
first chartered by Henry IV *c.* 1407-8. They were primarily engaged in foreign trade, chiefly with the Netherlands, and they

exercised a monopoly of the export of woolen cloth. They were frequently attacked during the seventeenth century, and Lilburne is here carrying on a developing economic attitude. He goes to great length on the subject in his *Innocency and Truth Justified* (pp. 48-62). Notwithstanding the general opposition to such monopolies, Parliament on October 11, 1643, passed "An Ordinance . . . for the upholding the government of the Fellowship of Merchant Adventurers of England to the better Maintenance of the Trade of Cloathing and wollen manufacture of the Kingdome" (reprinted by Lingelbach). Fearing that their interests would be jeopardized by the king's efforts for raising revenue, the Adventurers had sided with Parliament, and in the early stages of the struggle Parliament had been indebted to them for loans (*Commons Journal*, III, 364, 405, cited by Pease, *Leveller Movement*, pp. 118-119). The company was, perhaps in consequence, confirmed in its monopoly and in its right to administer an oath which, under approval by both Houses, bound its members to faithful observance of all its regulations (reprinted by Lingelbach). In addition to Pease, cited above, see Cunningham, *Growth of English Industry and Commerce*, II, 214-234; and Lingelbach, *The Merchant Adventurers of England: Their Laws and Ordinances*, Philadelphia, 1902; and *The Internal Organization of the Merchant Adventurers*, Philadelphia, 1902.

l. 19   mischievousnesse you may] mischievousnesse of which you may. See Errata, p. 305.

l. 20   a late discourse] *A Discourse consisting of Motives for the enlargement and freedome of Trade, Especially that of Cloth, and other Woolen Manufacturers, Engrossed at present Contrary to the Law of Nature, and the Lawes of this Kingdome. By a Company of private men who stile themselves Merchant Adventurers* (April 23), 1645. This anonymous tract was probably written by Thomas Johnson, who some months later published a very similar tract, *A Plea for Free-Mens Liberties: or the Monopoly of the Eastland Marchants anatomized (which will also serve to set forth the unjustnesse of the Marchant-Adventurers Monopoly,) and Proved illegall, unnaturall, irrationall* (January 26), 1646. Both tracts serve as excellent illustrations of the manner in which attacks on privilege, whether in religion, politics or trade, ran on similar lines.

l. 32   are as culpable] are culpable. See Errata, p. 305.

268, l. 7   Monopoly of Printing] For the Stationers' Company and the regulations concerning printing before and after the Long Parliament, see Vol. I, pp. 9, 46-47.

l. 19   bublick] publick. See Errata, p. 305.

269, l. 12   *Oxford Aulicus*] See p. 108, note.

271, l. 5   Ordinance lately made] See p. 77, note.

l. 36   Petitions] Available records refer to petitions in agitation at this time rather than to petitions already being presented to Parliament. The Thomason Catalogue lists several such petitions submitted and published in 1646 and 1647. Lilburne may be referring here particularly to petitions probably at this time being circulated in Hertfordshire and Buckinghamshire. Overton alluded to this agitation in his *Ordinance for Tithes dismounted* (December 29), 1645. The petition itself was brought to the bar of the House on May 5, 1646, by a deputation of upwards of two thousand persons from Hertfordshire and Buckinghamshire, and at about the same time was published *The Husbandmans Plea against Tithes, or Two Petitions presented unto the House of Commons by divers Freeholders of Hertfordshire* (May 25). This pamphlet is especially interesting for the detailed information it supplies concerning the economic predicament of farmers together with the claim to relief from tithes on grounds of natural right.

273, l. 18   *evill good*] *evill good, and good evill.* See Errata, p. 305.

l. 19   *bitter.*] *bitter. Job* 14.4. Who can bring a clean thing out of an uncleane? not one. read 25.4 and *Psalm.* 51.5. See Errata, p. 305.

274, l. 10   *Lilburnes* lying in Newgate] Arrested July 19, 1645, by order of the House on the occasion of the presentation of charges by the Salters Hall committee against Speaker Lenthall (see p. 264, note), Lilburne was brought before a committee of the House on July 24. He refused to answer questions put to him by the committee until he should be informed of the charges against him and denounced as illegal the action of the House in committing him without specifying the reason. He was therefore recommitted. He immediately published a pamphlet, *The Copy of a Letter . . . to a friend* (August 9), and was ordered by the House to be examined again. Again he refused to answer questions and was remanded to Newgate. On August 11 the House ordered him to be held for trial at the next quarter session.

l. 16   to prison] *to prison without a cause shewed.* See Errata, p. 305.

l. 18   Imprisonment] Imprisonment *to force him to commit a crime.* See Errata, p. 305.

l. 26   to make] make. See Errata, p. 305.

l. 29   Lilburne adds a lengthy postscript (see pp. 306-307) which he directs the reader to insert at this point.

275, l. 2   *Manchesters* treachery] Cromwell as lieutenant general under Manchester came to differ with his superior officer, who in his opinion leaned too much toward the Presbyterians under the evil influence of Major General Crawford. He severely criticized Manchester's inactivity and incapacity at the second Battle of Newbury and in the campaign which followed the capture of York. On November 25, 1644, Cromwell attacked him on these grounds before the House of Commons, supporting the accusation by an account of Manchester's operations from the Battle of Marston Moor to the relief of Donnington Castle. Manchester replied by a defense of his generalship and the accusation that Cromwell had used offensive and incendiary language against the nobility, the Westminster Assembly, the Scots and others. The Commons appointed a committee to investigate Manchester and the Lords another to investigate Cromwell. The latter characteristically drew back from his charge against Manchester in order to concentrate on the attainment of a professional army led by a professional general. On December 9 he urged the House to consider the remedies rather than the causes of the late miscarriages and reduced his charge against Manchester to one of accidental oversight, which he begged the House not to press. He insisted on the removal of members of both Houses from military command and on putting the army "into another method." The result was the adoption of the Self-Denying Ordinance and the organization of the New Model under Fairfax. By a series of circumstances Cromwell, though a member of the House, was eventually retained in his command at the request of Fairfax.

l. 14   streightned] strengthned. See Errata, p. 305.

l. 20   Master *Mussenden* and Mr. *Wolley*] For Lilburne's account of his affair with Colonel King, see especially his *Innocency and Truth* and *The Just Mans Justification.* Lincolnshire was added, September 20, 1643, by Parliamentary ordinance to the

Eastern Association. Since it had been so recently won from the Royalists, Cromwell and Manchester appointed Col. Edward King, a Lincolnshire man, governor of Boston and Holland. Lilburne was appointed, October 7, to be major under King and instructed by Cromwell to report in case he found King or anyone else "acting against Salus Poppuli." Lilburne says that he remained on good terms with his commanding officer until the latter's chaplain "set them by the ears." Consequently Lilburne received none of the money sent by the Committee of Lincoln at the time of the siege of Newark for paying King's soldiers. Lilburne presently preferred charges against King to Cromwell and Manchester, accusing him of pride and arrogance, of having treacherously lost Crowland, of having put Holland in jeopardy, of having failed to pay his soldiers with the money provided by the Committee of Lincoln, and of having been in large part the cause of the defeat at Newark, March 22, 1644. He attempted to have King court-martialed, and Mr. Archer and others of the Committee of Lincoln "drew up a very heinous charge against King and laboured hard for a trial." The officers of the town of Boston urged Cromwell to influence Manchester to try King before a Council of War. After the failure of these attempts, "Mr. Mussenden, Mr. Wolley and divers others of the Committee of Lincoln did exhibit Articles of a very high nature to the House of Commons against him" in August, 1644. Lilburne annexes to *The Just Mans Justification* a copy of these articles. He further accused King of conniving at his arrest in July, 1645 (see above) because King knew that he was a main witness to many of the charges contained in the articles, and then after his discharge of having him arrested April 14, 1646, upon a trumped-up suit for £2,000 damages for having called King a traitor. According to the Commons Journal, Manchester was, March 3, 1645, requested to recall King's commission by request of the House.

276, l. 13 *Musgrave*] John Musgrave, a gentleman of Cumberland, served for a time in the Parliamentary armies, but quarreled with the Parliamentary authorities in Cumberland, by whom he was arrested on several occasions as a malcontent. By the beginning of 1645 he was in London addressing petitions to Parliament in accusation of various persons but particularly of Richard Barwis, a member of the House. The House referred the matter to a committee and finally sent Musgrave to the Fleet, October 28, 1645, for refusing to answer questions. From prison he put forth three violent pamphlets, *A Word to the Wise* (January 26), 1646, *Another Word to the Wise* (February 20), and *Yet Another Word to the Wise* (October 1). After his release in January, 1647, he continued further his quarrelsome career.

277, l. 1   *Durham*] Sir Henry Vane the elder (1589-1655), secretary of state to Charles I, was one of the judges in Star Chamber who tried Lilburne in 1637, but sided with Parliament and was made Lord Lieutenant of Durham. The county fell at once under the control of the Royalists, and Vane exercised no real authority there until the end of 1644. Lilburne, himself from Durham and hostile to the Vanes, accused Sir Henry of causing the loss of the county by negligence and treachery, but the charge met no acceptance from Parliament (see *The Resolved Mans Resolution*, pp. 13-18). Lilburne also accused Vane of breaking up the Short Parliament in order to protect his own monopoly of gunpowder, of joining Parliament against the king out of self-interest, and of continuing to aid Charles by sending arms through his servants, Conyers and Dingley, to the Earl of Newcastle. Lilburne's father, Richard Lilburne, as well as his uncle, George Lilburne, to whom Lilburne refers just below, were both involved in these accusations against Vane.

279, l. 16   *Gurney . . . Gardner*] Sir Richard Gurney, whom Charles later made a baron, was Lord Mayor of London at the outbreak of the troubles and a Royalist. The citizens complained to the Commons of his conduct. In July, 1642, he was impeached for having published the king's commission of array in the City, and in the following month condemned to prison by the House of Lords. Sir Thomas Gardner, also a Royalist, was Recorder of London and a defeated candidate for the Long Parliament. He succeeded in joining the king at Oxford and in October, 1643, was nominated by Charles to be solicitor general. As Mayor Gurney had been faithless to Parliament at an earlier point, so Lilburne is attempting to establish that the Mayor and Common Council are in 1645 faithless to the people's interest. They were in fact Presbyterian in their sympathies, as was shown in the ensuing year by their *Humble Remonstrance and Petition* (May 26) for the adoption of the Directory and the suppression of heresy.

280, l. 30   debarr] debarred

283, l. 12   Captaine *Cob*] The administration of Upper Bench Prison by Sir John Lenthall as Marshall was investigated in 1653 by the Committee for Prisons. Among the charges against Lenthall at that time was one to the effect that "one captain William Cob who was a prisoner in the Upper Bench Prison and an active man in the Discovery of Sir John Lenthall's Treachery to the State was confidently believed to be poisoned by the Servants of the said Sir John Lenthall" (*Commons Journal* VII, 303).

284, ll. 6, 7   *Violet . . .* Sir *Bassell Brooke*] These were figures in an unsuccessful Royalist plot. In December, 1643, Colonel Reade, a Catholic, escaped from the Tower to Oxford and urged the king to open a correspondence with Sir Basil Brook. The latter, a Catholic who had risen to favor under Portland's protection in Charles's happier years, had been negotiating with the Catholics for their support of the throne. He agreed to do his best to win the City to the king's cause. One of his main instruments was Violet, a Royalist goldsmith who had been in prison for failing to pay his share of contributions to the Parliamentary cause. Brook had charge of the contributions made by English Catholics in support of the king's war against the Scots at the outbreak of the troubles, and was implicated in an alleged plot to create division between Parliament and the City and to prevent the advance of the Scots into England. He was committed by the Commons to the Tower, January 6, 1644.

l. 34   *Bastwick*] Bastwick was instrumental in bringing about Lilburne's arrest in July, 1645. His "late book" was *A Just Defence of John Bastwick* (August 30), 1645.

288, l. 34   *those Parliament men*] The Self-Denying Ordinance, which finally passed the Lords on April 3, 1645, required members of Parliament to resign within forty days any posts which they held under the Parliament. Lilburne is here objecting that obedience to the ordinance has not been exacted of Sir Henry Mildmay, Sir Henry Vane, Oliver St. John, Cornelius Holland and others.

291, l. 37   Withers] *Letters of Advice touching the Choice of Knights and Burgesses for the Parliament*, second edition (September 3), 1645; first edition (November 2), 1644.

292, l. 15   *Vox Pacifica*] *Vox Pacifica: A Voice tending to the Pacification of Gods Wrath*, 1645, a poem in four cantos by George Wither.

293, l. 4   *Some Advertisements*] *Some Advertisements for the New*

Election of Burgesses for the House of Commons (September 20),
1645, attributed by the *Dictionary of National Biography* to
George Wither.

294, ll. 7-37   Was ever so desperate a wound given to the Lawes, Liberties and properties, as the predetermined judgement of Ship-mony.
Who gave that blow? Judges. What were they? Theeves *cum*
privilegio Rege majestatis, who bought Justice by wholesale, and
sold it by Retaile? Who assisted them? Lawyers, who undertaking
to pleade for their Clyants against it, (pretending one thing, and
doing another thing) for the most part; and betrayed the Cause,
all to get favour and preferment; and yet such proceedings were
both against the Judges, and the *Coronation Oath*; upon an ex-
trajuditiall opinion collusively given: (for saith the Record)
Sacramentum Domini Regis erga populum suum bibent ad cus-
todiendum; But our Judges, (though more wicked) have the hap-
pinesse to live in a more wicked age, and out live their crimes, paying onely a small part by way of fine: and enjoying the rest of
their stollen treasures: and after they had made Peace as devouring
as warre, and the Law as cruel as the Sword; who's that is not a
better Christian then these Brothers of the *Coyfe*, brothers in evill:
will not cry out with *Epicures*, that God takes no more care what
men doe on this earthly balke, then man doth what *Ants* doe on an
Emmet-hill; when *Verres*: (being *Consull* of *Cicily*,) had pilled
that *Province*, and (other *Pro-Consulls*, and *Pro-Pretors* were
punished for lesser Extortions) he laughing at their foolish moderation, vaunted to his Brother *Tymarkedes*: that he had got
anough to buy the friendship of the *Senate*, and commendation, of
a rich and Honourable man: So our Judges enjoy their crimes, and
the prize and reward of them: Nay, they grow fatt and prosper
upon the anger of God and man, whilest this Land groanes under
the sad weight of the *Sword, Pestilence*, and famine, the effects of
their injustice: but through whose favour is it they have not
expiated their Crimes with their blood: and washed away the
Guilt of the Land; but the *Lawyers*? who wisely consider it may
be their own Case another day.

l. 8   Ship-mony]   Charles I issued writs for the collection of ship
money in October, 1634, and August, 1635. John Hampden, refusing to pay, was brought to trial in 1637. Seven of the twelve judges
at the trial, headed by Finch, Chief Justice of the Common Pleas,

gave judgment for the crown and five for Hampden. Lilburne probably had also in mind the fact that, before the case was decided, Charles obtained a written opinion signed by ten of the judges to the effect that in time of national danger, of which the crown was sole judge, ship money might be levied on all parts of the country.

295, l. 3   Heretofore

ll. 8-10   Author . . . Antidote] As part of his contention for the supremacy of Parliament in all matters of church government, Prynne expressed his Erastian views on excommunication in his *Foure serious Questions of Grand Importance* (August 23), 1645. He was answered by an anonymous tract, *An Antidote against foure dangerous Quaeries* (September 2) and by George Walker in *A Brotherly and Friendly Censure* (September 10).

l. 12   disputes, for] disputes for,

l. 32   *Helpe to the Right understanding*] See Vol. III, pp. 189-201.

296, l. 2   of the

l. 3   who

l. 13   that late letter] *The Copy of a Letter from Lieutenant Colonell John Lilburne, to a Friend* (July 25), 1645. See Vol. I, p. 99.

l. 15   *Englands Misery*] *Englands Miserie, and Remedie in a Judicious Letter from an Utter-Barrister to his speciall Friend, concerning Lieutenant Colonel Lilburn's Imprisonment in Newgate* (September 14), 1645. Thomason notes on the title-page "Lilbournes owne."

297, l. 1   *according*] *according to*. See Errata, p. 305.

l. 2   Englands Cordiall Physick] *Englands Cordiall Physick to cure all her diseases, recover her lawes, peace, freedomes, and avoid all assesments within . . . two moneths* 1645.

l. 21   Bibles] According to the records in the Journals of the Commons and of the Lords, it would seem that, taking advantage of the scruples of the Assembly, the Stationers did acquire a practical monopoly over the selling of Bibles and raised their prices. On May 31, 1644, the Assembly complained to the Commons of errors in Bibles printed abroad. The House ordered the Committee for Printing to seize and suppress all such Bibles and consider some course to prevent their importation and sale. The Stationers Company petitioned, July 10, 1644, for the apprehension of certain persons as delinquents "to answer their contempts to the Ordinance of Parliament, in selling and venting Bibles, imported from beyond seas, wherein are many erroneous Faults in the Printing it." The House passed a resolution for an ordinance, August 20, 1645, that "no foreign impression of any English Bibles, imported from beyond Seas, shall be put to Sale, in any Parts of this Kingdom, until they have been viewed, perused and allowed by the Assembly of Divines, or such as they shall appoint."

l. 26 *mount*

l. 38 *vomite*

298, l. 18 *Tabernable] Tabernacle*

l. 23] Cnsider] Consider. See Errata, p. 305.

299, ll. 7-8 *then then] then thou*

l. 23 *lay wait] lay in wait*

l. 25 *houses*

300, l. 20 *Hunscott]* See Vol. I, p. 111 note.

l. 27 & neer

ll. 29-36 And none being in the House, but an old Gentle-woman at that time, whom they much frighted; as they did a young Gentle-woman in another place, to the great danger of her life (insomuch that she cryeth out in her extreame Fever, *Hunscott Hunscott*,) they ranne up into the Chambers, & stole out of his wives Drawers, divers pieces of her Child-bed linnen and such other things as they pleased, and refused to shew the Old-woman what they had stollen, though she earnestly intreated them.

301, l. 16 Is there] If there were. See Errata, p. 305.

302, l. 4 if

l. 22 working

l. 36 early

l. 37 bread

305, ll. 19-23 *And what will ye doe in the day of Visitation; and in the desolation which shall come from farre? to whom will ye seek for help? and where will ye leave your glory? Without me they shall bow down under the Prisoners, and they shall fall under the slaine, for all this his anger is not turned away, but his hand is stretched out still.*

307, l. 24 Prinnes . . . *Soveraign Power]* This summary of the contents of the Appendix to the *Fourth Part of the Soveraigne Power of Parliament* (August 28), 1643, by William Prynne is quoted verbatim from the work itself.

311, l. 14 The Great Charter] The Great Charter refers to Magna

Charta. The Petition of Right was the expression of popular aspirations for liberty in 1628. The abolition of Star Chamber, to which
the king assented, July 5, 1641, was one of the first objectives of the
popular party in the Long Parliament. The Protestation, which
the members of both houses subscribed May 4, 1641, and which
was then circulated in the City for signature by the people, represented an effort by the Parliamentary leaders to align popular
opinion against the Royalists. It exacted of its signers the somewhat equivocal declaration that they would maintain and defend
"the true Reformed Protestant Religion expressed in the doctrine of
the Church of England" and "according to the duty of my alle-
giance, his Majesty's Royal person, honour and estate, as also the
power and privileges of Parliament, the lawful rights and liberties
of the subject, and every person that maketh the protestation in
whatsoever he shall do in the lawful pursuance of the same." The
Covenant was a similar vow intended to cement the Scotch and
English revolutionary parties in opposition to the king and the
prelates. It exacted a pledge to preserve the Church of Scotland
and to reform the Church of England according to the word of
God "and the example of the best reformed Churches." The Covenant came to be regarded by the Scotch and the Presbyterians as a
pledge to establish Presbyterianism in England; by the radicals of
all sorts, who nevertheless took advantage as we see Walwyn doing
here of its equivocal language, as an attempt to snare the consciences of the people. It was drawn up in August, 1643, and
shortly afterward subscribed by both houses and by the Westminster
Assembly. In the following February an attempt was made to
impose it upon all Englishmen. It was supposed to be required of
all soldiers and was in practice exacted of all officers in the army.

312, ll. 24-39   And this hath been my course and practice in things of
that nature for almost a score of yeares, whoever have been the
Judges, whether Parliament, King, Counsell-board, Starr Chamber,
High Commission, Kings-bench, or any Judicatory, yea whatever
the accuser, or the accused, the judgement or punishment hath
been; I have taken this my just and necessary liberty; for having
read, observed, debated and considered both ancient and latter
times, the variations and changes of Governments and Governors,
and looking upon the present with an impartiall judgement, I still
find a necessity of the same my accustomed watchfullnesse, it never

being out of date; [the more my hearts grief] for worthy and good men (nay the most publique spirited men) to suffer for well doing, unto whom only is promised the blessing and the heavenly Kingdome: *Mat.* 5.10.

Your suffering at present, is become every good mans wonder; for they all universally conclude your faithfullnesse and zeale to the publique weale to be such, as no occasion or tentation could possibly corrupt, and the testimonies you have given thereof to be so great, as greater could not be.

313, l. 3   Cromwell] For Lilburne's account of this affair, see his *Innocency and Truth*. It appears that, when Lilburne withdrew from the army early in 1645 and found himself "robd of his trade," he drew up a petition to the House of Commons for arrears of pay and reparation for the injuries done him by Star Chamber in 1637. Failing to get this petition read in the House, he had it printed and copies distributed to members. He then rode down to see Cromwell in the country and secured from him a letter strongly recommending him and his cause to the attention of the House.

315, l. 13   yon] you

ll. 33-34   no authoritie in the world can over-rule without palpable sinne

ll. 35-36   therein mentioned

316, ll. 6-13   For the Parliament is ever at libertie to make the People more free from burthens and oppressions of any nature, but in things appertaining to the universall Rules of common equitie and justice, all men and all Authority in the world are bound.

This Parliament was preserved and established, by the love and affections of the people, because they found themselves in great bondage and thralldome both spirituall and temporall;

l. 16   but

317, ll. 20-21   one only . . . *Martine*] Walwyn attributes the exclusion of Henry Marten from Parliament to Prynne. Marten, one of the most extreme and fiery members of the popular party in the Long Parliament, was suspended from the House of Commons and imprisoned in the Tower from August 19 to September 2, 1643. He was not readmitted to Parliament until January 6, 1646.

ll. 28-38   The Poyson of Asps is under that wicked mans tongue, with which he laboureth alwaies to poyson Scripture (mixing it figuratively) in his discourse to corrupt, sinister, and unworthy ends, whose malice and hypocrisie (doubtlesse) will ere long discover him to all men.

And (I doubt not) but that same God that took a happie course with *Haman* and delivered *Mordecai* and all his people, will in your great necessity and his fittest opportunity, fight against all your enemies and deliver both you and all yours out of all your afflictions, at least, so to mitigate and sweeten them by supporting you under them, (or rather bearing of them with you,) that they shall prove to be exceeding joyes and consolations, to you and all that love you.

328, l. 10   othes] other

345(12), l. 13   his I did] this I did
         l. 15   vaine distinctions

354, l. 30   Remonstrance] The Grand Remonstrance was adopted by the House of Commons November 22, 1641. It charged the evil counselors of the king of a "malignant and pernicious design of subverting the fundamental laws and principles of government" and cited a long list of enormities committed by the royal government since the beginning of the reign sixteen years before. In this passage Overton is, of course, drawing the somewhat unwarrantable inference that Parliament had expressed in the Grand Remonstrance the intention of reforming the government according to the extreme ideas of the Levellers of 1646.

360, l. 1   *but wee] but wee say not*
     l. 5   *wee] were*
     l. 31   *comrany] company*

361, l. 38   entured] ventured

362, l. 29   invite
     l. 32   willfull

364, l. 14   *scarce free*
     l. 23   *comming in*

365, l. 6   *Turky Company*, and the *Adventerers*] For the Merchant Adventurers, see above, p. 267 and note. The Turkey or, as it was commonly called, the Levant Company, chartered under Elizabeth in 1581, exercised privileges for trade in the Near East similar to those enjoyed elsewhere by the Merchant Adventurers.

370, ll. 1-2   if a present *Parliament* be mistaken in their understandings, and doe things prejudiciall
      l. 31   *as for me*

375, l. 2   *Martin*] See above, p. 317 and note. Readmitted to Parliament in January, 1646, Marten was appointed in the autumn of the same year to be chairman of a committee appointed by the Commons to investigate the Lords' proceedings against Lilburne and Overton. From 1647 to 1649, though not in entire agreement with Lilburne, he allied himself with the Levellers. He was active in bringing about the execution of the king, at whose trial he served as one of the judges. After Charles the Second's proclamation to the regicides in 1660, he surrendered and was imprisoned for the rest of his life.

376, marginal note *See the defiance*] *A Defiance against all Arbitrary Usurpations* (September 9) and *An Arrow against all Tyrants* (October 12), 1647, were pamphlets in which Overton recorded the earlier stages of his controversy with the House of Lords.

378, l. 11   Gusts

379, l. 8   nature itselfe teaches

    l. 30   authority

    l. 36   execution

380, l. 4   hat] that

    l. 5   & as it is

    l. 33   rationally will] rationally I will

381, l. 35   as free

386, l. 1   their

    l. 2   in case

    l. 13   Sir *Edward Cooks*] Overton and the other Levellers leaned heavily upon the authority of Coke for their contention that Parliament could not rightly make statutes contrary to the common law. Sir Edward Coke (1552-1634), attorney general, judge, and legal writer, in his capacity as Chief Justice of the Common Pleas (appointed 1606), defended the common law against the absolutist doctrines of the clergy who argued that the ecclesiastical courts should have coördinate jurisdiction with the secular courts, the powers of both being held by delegation from the king. James was flattered by the clergy's views and, eager to carry into practice his exaggerated notion of the prerogative, gave them his strong support. Coke opposed him strenuously, resisting him in various other matters as well, and making an unsuccessful attempt to check the practice of the crown in consulting the judges extra-judicially. James's hostility finally effected Coke's removal from the bench in

1616. The latter appeared, however, as one of the leaders on the popular side in the Parliament of 1620. In Charles's first Parliament, 1625, Coke argued against the grant of tonnage and poundage. In that of 1628, he brought in the bill of liberties, out of which grew the Petition of Right. In that petition, he objected to the use of the phrase "sovereign power" as applied to the crown on the ground that it was a new and dangerous phrase unknown to Magna Charta and other statutes of freedom. His chief works are his *Reports* and his *Institutes of the Lawes of England*, the latter of which had been published in 1642 by order of the House of Commons. The second part of this work gave the text of various statutes from Magna Charta to James I with an extended commentary.

l. 31   derived] deprived
l. 37   into that
387, l. 35   crouch
399, l. 1   *free*

INDEX

ERRATA

Vol. II, p. 215: *Delete* IV
Vol. II, p. 271, l. 11: *For* Browe *read* Brome
Vol. III, p. 1, l. 7: *For* Volume II, IV *read* Volume II, page 215
Vol. III, p. 59: *Delete* II